D1079610

The Secret Place

The Secret Place

Finding quiet time in the presence of God

ANGUS BUCHAN

MONARCH
BOOKS

Oxford, UK & Grand Rapids, Michigan, USA

Text copyright © 2013 Angus Buchan
This edition copyright © 2014 Lion Hudson

The right of Angus Buchan to be identified as the author of this
work has been asserted by him in accordance with the Copyright,
Designs and Patents Act 1988.

All rights reserved. No part of this publication may be reproduced
or transmitted in any form or by any means, electronic or
mechanical, including photocopy, recording, or any information
storage and retrieval system, without permission in writing from
the publisher.

Published by Monarch Books
an imprint of
Lion Hudson plc
Wilkinson House, Jordan Hill Road,
Oxford OX2 8DR, England
Email: monarch@lionhudson.com
www.lionhudson.com/monarch

ISBN 978 0 85721 557 4

Originally published as *The Booth* by
Christian Art Publishers,
PO Box 1599, Vereeniging, 1930, RSA
This edition 2014

Acknowledgments
Scripture quotations are taken from the Holy Bible, New Living
Translation®, first edition. Copyright © 1996 by Tyndale House
Publishers, Inc., Carol Stream, Illinois 60188.
Lyrics on page 93 used by permission of Cornelis van Heyningen ©
2008 Home for a Heart Productions

A catalogue record for this book is available from the British
Library

Printed and bound in the UK, May 2014, LH26

Dedication

To all the intercessors of this world, and my wife, Jill, who is one of them. These folk really know about getting into that "special place" and waiting upon God.

I value them more than any other ministry.

Contents

Foreword
by Jill Buchan

The corner of Stafford Avenue was always busy. There was a small grocer's shop where Granddad bought his newspaper and pipe tobacco. Jars filled with coloured sweets stood in a line on the counter. Granddad always bought a few in a small paper bag. The doorbell rang continually as people walked in and out, cars and buses passing by on the main road.

Next to the grocer's shop was a bright red telephone booth. Sometimes I was allowed to go in with Grandma to make a telephone call. I loved to go inside The Secret Place with her because when she closed the heavy door and it clicked shut, we couldn't hear the sound of the traffic, the shop bell ringing, or people talking. The quiet was reminiscent of that of my home – next to the Luapula River in Africa. My parents worked at a leprosy hospital 11 kilometres from the Mbereshi mission station in Zambia.

I was eight years old and I could just see out of The Secret Place's lowest window pane. I would hear the coins clink in the phone box and Grandma would chat, say goodbye, and hang up the phone. Then she would open the door and close it behind us and we would walk back up the avenue.

This book is called *The Secret Place*. My prayer is that it would encourage many Christians to realise our need of a "booth" in our lives: a place where we can open the door, leave the concerns of this world outside, go in and close it, and find only the stillness of God's presence. There we can talk with Him, our Father; where noise, busyness, and voices demanding our attention cannot be heard.

It is in that place early every morning that we need to come to Jesus – before the day begins. There, should we look up to the fading night skies, we might still see a few last twinkling stars (or are they the twinkling lights of our heavenly home)? We need to quieten our hearts before the Father, maybe climb up onto His knee, lay a weary head against His heart, and hear His heartbeat, strong and full of life and love for us – a reminder that we were made for Him. There we receive His assurance, His peace, and His sustenance from His Word. We need to read and know the Word of God in these days so that we can know God's truth and be alert to deceptions.

At the moment, my "booth" is a small wooden desk just under a window, looking out onto an orchard. Tall trees grow beyond the trees, and fruit-eating birds and colourful butterflies flit amongst the trees. Morning by morning, often before the sun rises and I am alone with God, He speaks to me of His love, His plans, and His purposes for me.

He will do the same for all those who come to Him, to share our sorrows and our joys at any time of the day with Him. With overfull diaries and still more demands on our time, I am reminded of an old hymn sung by many over the years:

> *Jesus calls us: o'er the tumult*
> *Of our life's wild, restless sea,*
> *Day by day His sweet voice callest,*
> *Saying, "Christian, follow Me".*

God calls us to lie down in green pastures and by quiet pools from time to time, but as the necessity to spend more time in our booth with Jesus becomes greater, I pray that we will learn how to live and move and have our being in Him, our God.

As *The Secret Place* challenges us to realize our increasing dependence on God in a vital relationship with Him, it will become who we are – our love for Jesus and for all men. That will enable us to be found amongst those sent out by the Lord of the harvest, to bring in His precious souls. It's harvest time and Jesus Christ is coming again very soon. His word to us is still "watch and pray".

Preface

Finding Quiet Time
in the Presence of God

Many people have asked in recent times how I have a quiet time with God. They want to know how to hear from God, how He speaks to us. I was very privileged to have been invited to Jerusalem at the end of 2012 to be one of the speakers at the international conference at the Feast of Tabernacles. Accordingly, I looked into the meaning of the event, one of the oldest festivals in Jewish history.

Every year the Jews remember the time when God delivered them from slavery in Egypt, and how, for forty years, He protected them, fed them, and defended them. It is a national holiday in Israel, one that lasts for seven days. The people of Israel build little booths in their gardens to remind them of how God provided for them in their wanderings in the desert, when they lived in temporal dwellings (tabernacles). It is a time of great joy and celebration, and the people spend lots of time in these dwellings.

I really believe that this is one of the main reasons why the Jewish nation has survived through so many horrific attacks from the world. Many civilizations have tried to annihilate them from the face of the earth. They have survived because they remember what God has done for them in the past; He remains with them and will always be with them. He is a miracle-working God.

Having a quiet time with God every day is the very same principle: It's spending the first hours of the new day with Jesus, basically having fellowship with Him, speaking to Him, listening to that still small voice, saying, "This is the way..." It's spending time reading His living Word, the Bible, and then meditating on these encouragements and, if necessary, gentle rebukes.

Honestly, without time every morning spent in the presence of God, I would never make it. I find that the longer I walk with Jesus, the more time I desire to meet with Him in my closet – my separate place where there are no distractions or interferences from the world. The Lord soothes my nerves and quietens my spirit. He inspires my preaching and reminds me daily of my priorities: God first; my wife, Jill, next; then my children and grandchildren; and so on.

The more time you spend with a person, the more you become like that person. The disciples often couldn't find Jesus – He was always up the mountain, waiting on His Father. But when He came down, all heaven broke loose: the sick were healed; captives set free; miracles, signs, and wonders took place. This is what I believe the Father wants me to write about in more detail: becoming more like Jesus!

Chapter 1

This Busy World

In this busy world in which we are desperately trying to exist, to keep sane, to keep balanced, we need a place where we can rest, a place where we can gather ourselves: a getaway, somewhere we find peace; a place to regroup against the onslaught of a world that seems to have gone mad. So many people have asked me how I cope. The answer is very simple: by spending time with Father God each morning.

It is good having a quiet time each day and listening to that still small voice giving me peace. At the Feast of Tabernacles, where I was privileged to be a guest speaker in 2012, for the first time I realized what the festival was really about. It reminds the Jewish people of how God provided for them in the wilderness for forty years – their sandals never wore out, their clothes never fell to pieces, and God fed them all, every day, with manna from heaven!

The importance of The Secret Place

During the feast the Jews build a small little booth (called a "succoth") at the bottom of their gardens, from young poplar branches. They decorate these succoths with fruit, and live in them for seven days. It is a time to celebrate the bringing in of the produce of the fields, both fruit and grain, such as grapes, dates, olives, and so forth. However, the main reason is to remember that the Lord loved them and protected them in the wilderness.

I was so excited to hear about this wonderful festival, because that is exactly what Father God has shown me. He wants you and me to have a booth where He can speak to us unhindered by the hustle and bustle of this busy world in which we live. It needs to be a separate place where we can have uninterrupted fellowship together. He so wants to speak with us, and at the very same time the devil is hell bent on breaking off any communications we might have with our God. The most effective way for the devil to do this is by keeping us flat-out busy, with no place to be quiet, keeping us on the treadmill, to the extent that if we are not going full speed, we actually feel guilty.

This morning while sitting in my booth I had a visit from a dear son of mine in the Lord, who had come over from Europe to see his family in South Africa. He popped in to have a cup of coffee with me and gave me a photograph in a beautiful frame. It was of a little wooden house he had built in his garden – his little booth, the place where he spends time with God. I was very touched. This man has physically shown that he truly means business.

This son is an extremely busy man who works for the ministry of justice and holds a very senior position. In fact, he has the authority to make major adjustments to the penal code system, which could revolutionize the way prisoners are managed. It is an incredible opportunity for this young man to put into practice what Jesus has told us to do: to literally set the captives free.

The fact that this young man has gone to the extent of building a small wooden hut and placing it at the bottom of his garden tells me that he is serious about having a proper quiet time with Jesus every day. That means he is going to hear clearly from God, and will be given the faith and strength to implement God's directives. He could very well become our next modern day "Wilberforce" who was instrumental in abolishing the hellish slave trade. All this because he made a decision to have a proper quiet time with Jesus every day. He does this before going to work and making life-changing decisions that could not only affect thousands of prisoners sitting in Europe's jails, but also society at large. It cannot be stressed enough how time spent with God first thing in the morning can change a man's life, his outlook, and the impact he will have on society.

The art of patience

What I am just realizing in this life is that it takes more discipline to wait than it takes to keep doing things. As I grow older, this is a discipline I have to work very hard at if I am to fulfil God's call on my life and to finish the race strong!

One of the most significant testings for me is to wait in the departure lounge of an international airport. It's an excellent place and opportunity to exercise that discipline of waiting, an attitude of life that the world seems to have forgotten how to implement, especially in first world countries. In third world countries, people have little or no problem with waiting for a bus to take them from a rural farming area to the nearest town. They can wait a day or even two and they just take it in their stride. But in first world countries, if a train or aeroplane is five or ten minutes late, all pandemonium breaks loose.

So as I sit and wait for my connecting flight I have up to nine hours to occupy myself with whatever I choose to do. Watching people from different walks of life, different cultures and ethnic groups really fascinates me. I observe people from Asian, African, and European backgrounds; old people, young people – watching their mannerisms, how they dress, what food they like to eat and, most of all, how they choose to occupy their time while they wait for their flights.

Jesus speaks to us clearly about "redeeming the time" – in other words, not wasting it on trivial issues. Once again, we as believers are just so privileged to have a personal relationship with the living God, and so we don't ever have need to fill in the time with arbitrary things that have no heavenly or earthly value. We have no need to ever feel lonely, even when we travel in a foreign country, because He travels with us. Life for me has become so full and exciting since I've become a follower of Jesus! He has given my life new meaning.

While I sit in departure lounges, I meditate on the many opportunities that the Lord has opened up. I ask, "Where to from here, Jesus?" I am reminded of the time when I had just left a meeting and was sitting with my son in the car outside. The host came out and pleaded with us to come back into the service, because a woman was waiting for prayer for healing. She had been waiting all night and had driven some 144 kilometres. She was anxious for me to pray for her to be healed. During the service I'd been speaking about vision and told the listeners I wouldn't be

> We have no need to ever feel lonely, because He travels with us.

praying for the sick that night, hence the urgent prayer request.

So we went straight back into the hall. Most of the people had gone, although there were still a few left. We anointed this dear lady with oil and in the name of Jesus Christ, the great Healer, we asked her to rise up and walk. That dear lady, without any hesitation whatsoever, got out of her wheelchair and started walking. The people who were there went ballistic. I asked her to stay for the evening service and to give her testimony, to show the people what Jesus had done for her. She agreed and someone very kindly put her up in their home that night. Well, that evening, when the lady walked the full length of the hall and back again, the crowd went crazy! For weeks afterward, I received phone calls to say that people all over the district were talking about what happened, with much joy and jubilation.

This is an example of what happened during a trip overseas. Instead of sitting for nine hours doing nothing but getting stressed and frustrated, I use the time to pray and give thanks to God for using me, remembering all the great things He has done. Then, with great expectation, I wait upon

> I use the time to pray and give thanks to God for using me.

Him to find out, "Where to from here?" So you see how easy it is for a believer to pass valuable time, waiting to hear from God for new inspiration, new direction. It is such an exciting way of life, and I am so honoured that Jesus has given me this opportunity.

Quiet time

Often people ask me how much time I spend in the presence of God every morning. Well, the answer is "as much time as I possibly can". The reason is quite simple: it is because I have a relationship with Jesus Christ and it is not an effort for me to get out of bed in the morning and to spend time with Him simply because I love Him so much. Spending time with God should never be a huge discipline.

I remember when I fell in love with my wife, Jill. In those days we didn't have much money. We would go to the park, buy an ice cream, and sit down on a bench. We would eat our ice cream and just talk about lots of different things. Sometimes we didn't even talk; we just stared into each other's eyes – you know what it's like when you fall in love. We didn't have to be told that we needed to spend time together.

I could never wait to see Jill. She stayed in town, I on a farm, and the only time that I could actually meet her would be on the weekend or a Wednesday night. My whole week would be geared towards that special time. I had it all planned out: I would be in my Sunday best, groomed and ready to meet her. I'd make sure my car was washed and dust free; I'd ensure my hair was cut or looking smart because I wanted to impress her.

It was never a burden for me to spend time with a lady whom I loved so much. I might add, as I get older it's even more desirable for me to be with her. The more I leave her, the harder it is, because the road that I am walking now – the route that God has chosen for me – means that we don't see each other as often as we did when I was farming full time. Jill does not travel with me often, and this work that I am doing – although I live for it and love telling people about Jesus – can be quite demanding, to say the least. So when we are at home together we don't have to have entertainment; we don't have to go on holiday with five or ten other families. Just my wife and myself is quite sufficient.

Likewise, with the Lord Jesus Christ, when you have met Him as your personal Lord and Saviour and that love relationship has developed, it is actually not a problem and no burden at all to get up in the morning before the busy day starts and just spend time with Him. I do it gladly.

I cannot face the day without first spending time with the Master. Sometimes it is extremely hard, especially if I am in a country with a different time frame – it sometimes seems like the middle of the night, yet it might be midday. It is rather disorientating. I preach at different times, but still I am determined to meet with the Lord in a personal way. Obviously I meet with Him all the time; He is in my conversation constantly, the One whom I tell people about, and yet there has to be that intimate, one-on-one time. It is like spending time with your husband or your wife – when you are with them and having a social gathering, it's wonderful. Your spouse is with you, but there has to be a time when it is just the two of you. That intimacy is so important for a successful marriage and so it is in our walk with the Lord. If there is no intimacy – no special relationship – then it will not last.

People always talk about getting to know the Bible, but I would like to suggest that you get to know the Author first. Then the Bible becomes a reality. You see, you can go to Israel and it is a wonderful place, but if you have never met the Man from Galilee personally – if you don't have an intimate relationship with Him – it is just another historical place. It is like going to Rome to see the

Coliseum or going to Egypt to see the pyramids – a wonderful experience, but that's where it ends.

Now when you know Jesus as your personal Lord and Saviour, you become extremely emotional when you go to Israel, because when you walk up the Via Dolorosa (the "Way of Sorrows"), you can imagine your best Friend carrying that cross and suffering because of the sin of the world.

> You need to ask yourself, *Do I really know Jesus Christ?*

When you go to Gethsemane and you see how He sweated drops of blood for you and me, then it becomes very moving. And I want to tell you that every time I come back from Israel (and I have been there a number of times now), I am never refreshed – I am always exhausted emotionally and spiritually because it has become such a reality to me. My life is enriched and the Bible becomes so much more real.

If you have to get out of bed because your pastor, or your father, your brother, or your husband says you must, then I want to say to you that you need to challenge yourself. You need to ask yourself, *Do I really know Jesus Christ?* I have never been told by anybody, since the day I was born again, that I need to get up and have my quiet time. No matter whether I am on a Christian camp, on an agricultural tour, or just at the farm, I get up because I want to hear from the Lord.

Hearing from God

That brings up a very interesting point: hearing from God. What does that actually entail? What does it mean?

How do you hear from Him? How does He speak to you? How do you get direction from Him? Well, I can only tell you how it is for me. Obviously I have learnt from the spiritual fathers that have gone before us and this is how it works with me: I start off first and foremost by reading my Bible, and I read it in the first person. In other words, if we take Psalm 23 as an example – "The Lord is my Shepherd" – the way I read it is: "The Lord is Angus's shepherd, Angus shall not want." Then it becomes very personal and real to me.

Secondly, I read the Bible systematically. I do not believe in just opening up the Bible at any place and putting your finger on a verse and hoping for the best. To me that is like Russian roulette and you can get badly injured by doing this. I read the Bible systematically every single day. I have a notebook and everything that God tells me through that Scripture I write down. For example, I'll start in the Psalms (the Old Testament) and then I'll start in the New Testament in the Gospel of John, because it's nice and easy reading and very encouraging. I will read a portion every day; some days I will read a chapter, some days it might be ten verses. I will read it maybe more than once and then write down in my "quiet time book" – normally a diary – what the Lord has said to me that day. Because I am a slow learner, when I write something down, I remember it.

Because I am doing about eleven programmes a week for television at the moment, people often ask me, "How do you get so many messages to preach?" Well, it's quite simple: I get the messages straight from the throne room of grace, fresh out of the oven like a fresh loaf of bread. As God speaks that Word to me, I relate it to the people and that is why it works – because it has nothing to do with me.

God often speaks to me through the Scripture verses I write down. I might be seeking Him for a specific answer and I would just continue to read my Bible methodically. The Lord might speak to me not once, not twice, but as many times as I desire to confirm what it is that He wants to say to me. There is no luck involved. It is actually very simple: just listen to the Word of the Lord.

In the Father's presence

Jesus was continually found up the mountain. Often the disciples would come and ask, "Lord, where have You been? People are waiting for You." He would never rush His time with His Father, because He knew that without His Father's input, He would have nothing to say.

When we have these huge men's conferences, I am possibly the loneliest man there, because I don't spend time socializing – I spend time in The Secret Place, hearing

> I don't spend time socializing – I spend time in The Secret Place, hearing from God.

from God so that I can relate a message that is relevant and of importance for these men to take home with them. The social part comes after the conference, when I go and visit those men on a one-on-one basis.

The Lord Jesus Christ is jealous for your company and mine; He does not want to share us with everybody else. Often I will take time in the morning and maybe not even say anything but wait and get my spirit into tune with the Lord. It's no good rushing in and rushing out – I don't believe God will speak to us under such circumstances.

I want to ask you, as you read this book, would you be prepared to share your heart with someone who you knew was just dying to get going, saying, "Hurry up, hurry up. What is it that you want to know?" I know what you would say, the same thing that I would: "Don't worry, we'll talk about it some other time."

God has taught me that when somebody comes to speak to me out of the crowd, I have to give that person my full attention, and sometimes people are offended by that. They think they are more important than the person I am speaking with, who might happen to be a street sweeper, an usher, a car guard, or whatever. I am prepared to give him or her my full attention, because they have asked me. And the other person, who might be the CEO of a large organization, must wait until I am finished. People are very important to me, as you and I are important to the Lord, so don't try to divide your time with God. Take that mug of coffee or tea, and go into your office, your little room, or wherever it is that you will be undisturbed. Quietly drink your coffee or tea and just wait and listen to God. Listen to some music if need be. Quieten your spirit, open your heart, and God will speak to you through the Scriptures.

> Quieten your spirit, open your heart, and God will speak to you through the Scriptures.

I have never had the privilege of hearing God speak to me audibly, but I want to tell you that He speaks to me through the Scriptures, sometimes more audibly than anybody else. He also speaks to me through nature. I am a jogger and I like to run. I am slow, but I like to go for an early morning run. Sometimes I use a headlight and while I am running I will open my heart. God will start to speak to my heart and minister to me and refresh my soul. This is especially important when I am away from home, because I am a person who gets extremely homesick. My quiet time is even more precious because it comforts my soul until I get back to my wife and family.

Once I have completed reading the New Testament and the Old Testament, and have written down in my diary what God impressed upon me, I normally use a daily reading book, or devotional. I get a Scripture and godly encouragement from some well-renowned author. I write that down as well and then I start to pray. As a new believer I was taught a simple method of praying in a constructive manner using the acronym ACTS.

A path to prayer

A brother of mine wrote down the word "ACTS" in the margin and next to the "A" he put Adoration. This is the time to adore the Lord in the morning, to give Him thanks for a new day; to praise Him that you are alive, that your family is alive, that it is a beautiful new morning. There are so many things to praise Him for – the promise that He will never leave us nor forsake us; the fact that He is the same yesterday, today, and forever.

When you have finished that time of adoration then you go to "C": Confession. This is the time to repent before the Lord, to ask God to forgive you for the way you messed up the day before. Maybe you lost your temper with your family unintentionally; maybe it's something you've neglected to do; maybe you have offended the

Lord in some area. Ask forgiveness and the Lord will forgive you. He says in 1 John 1:9: *"If we confess our sins He is faithful and just to forgive us our sins and to cleanse us from all unrighteousness."*

After confession comes the letter "T", for Thanksgiving. We should thank God that our names are written in the Lamb's Book of Life. It doesn't matter how hard we work. It's not about that – it's about His grace, His undeserved loving-kindness, that gives us the opportunity to call ourselves His children. We can thank Him for our family and loved ones; for new opportunities in life. There are so many things to be grateful for.

When you finish thanksgiving, the next letter is "S", which stands for Supplication. Pray for your loved ones. Often in a meeting people will come and say, "What can I do for you?" My answer is always, "Please pray for me. I don't want anything else. I don't want your money, but I want prayer."

Pray for others

The Bible says in James 5:16, *"The effective, fervent prayer of a righteous man avails much."* When we start to pray for others, God does something in our own hearts. Especially pray for your enemies, something that is often the hardest

> When we start to pray for others, God does something in our own hearts.

thing to do. Pray for those who say evil about you, pray for those who have turned their back on you, who have falsely accused you. Pray for them as Jesus prayed for His disciples, knowing full well they were going to betray Him, run away, and leave Him. Still He prayed for them.

Then, when I am finished doing this, I normally have a list of names that I pray for. I have many spiritual sons whom I am mentoring and I try to pray for them individually each day, that God may undertake for them. After praying for others, go out and face your day and I guarantee it will be wonderful, because the Bible says, *"If God is for us, who can be against us?"* (Romans 8:31). That is exactly what happens in my life. That intimacy doesn't stop in the prayer room. Not at all – it goes into the market place, onto the sports field, onto the farm, and, most importantly, onto the platform or the pulpit where you are preaching. People must see Jesus in you.

My dear friend, the greatest compliment that any person can ever pay you is when they say that they can see Jesus Christ in you. The only way this can happen is by spending time with the Master. There is simply no other way. You see, when you spend time with people, you become like them. The more time you spend in prayer, in reading the Word of God with other fellow believers, the more you become like Jesus Christ. You will start thinking the way the Lord thinks, and will start having compassion on the poor, the needy, the hungry, the lost, the elderly, the widows, and the orphans. As you support and bless them, God will honour you – it's as simple as that.

Of course there are many other advantages to having that time with the Master. He gives you clarity of thought – when you spend time in His presence, you start getting your priorities in order, you start realizing what's important in life and you don't get sidetracked. Instead of running around like a headless chicken, you start thinking soundly and start acting upon God's instruction.

It's vital to be a good example. You can tell your children till the cows come home that they need to spend time with God, but they will not do it until they see you doing the same. It's a wonderful thing when your kids get up in the morning and Dad is in his closet, his booth, spending time with the Lord. That will encourage them to do the same.

Healing through prayer

Come to Jesus when you are struggling with issues like depression, anxiety, fear, anger, or whatever it might be. When you spend time with the Lord, you will find soothing balm and guidance. The peace you find in your quiet time with God will help you more than any medicine. I have found that in my own life. Before I became a Christian, I regarded myself as a pretty good farmer, but there was many a time I couldn't sleep at night. I used to get so worried about the weather, the cost of things, the state of the country, and many other issues.

> When you spend time with the Lord, you will find soothing balm and guidance.

After I gave my life to Jesus, I started having these regular times with the Master and the Lord began to reassure me through His Word that He is in control of everything. The current government and the weather are not in control, because God is the weatherman. Then peace and tranquillity would come upon me and I would start thinking correctly. Then, of course, I began making the right decisions; people even perceived me as being a wise man. In actual fact, I was the same man I always was, but the Lord Jesus Christ became the captain of my ship. There are so many "spin-offs" to spending time in the presence of Almighty God.

I found that my relationship with others improved immeasurably: I became more patient and more understanding, looking at things not just from my point of view but from my fellow man's point of view as well. And with that tolerance came renewed respect; I found that men started to respect me more than ever before.

I discovered that my language started to change. Because I was aware of the presence of God in my life at all times, I had to brush up on my language. I had a very foul mouth before I became a believer, simply because my vocabulary was so limited. However, after spending time in God's presence, I didn't want, under any circumstance, to offend the Lord. As a result, I started to watch my tongue, and that overflowed to other people as well. In fact, I can honestly say to you that since the day that I was saved I have not blasphemed. I have shouted a lot, I must confess, and I am still working on that one, but I have never taken the Lord's name in vain or blasphemed in any way. It hasn't even been an effort for me; it's been the desire of my heart. You see, when you love somebody so much, there is no way that you want to offend them or in any way harm their reputation.

It's all about a personal relationship and that's what gets me up in the morning. It's what motivates me to spend time in the presence of Almighty God and it's what intensifies my first fruits of every morning: that friendship, that personality, that character I have grown to love and to know over the years.

Chapter 2

Rest

Many years ago I heard a very special story that I think highlights the necessity of spending quality time, and quantity time, with Jesus. Dr Stephen Alford, born in Zambia (the beautiful country I had the privilege of growing up in), was regarded as the "preacher's preacher". He told the true story of a dynamic young missionary who was called to start a mission station in the depths of the Congo jungle many years ago. This man single-handedly carved a beautiful mission station in the dense jungle, starting with a church, where he would preach faithfully every Sunday. Through him, many souls were brought to Christ Jesus as Saviour.

He would have midweek Bible study groups, and youth meetings every Friday night. In the meantime he built a school and taught the tribesmen how to read and write. He worked up to eighteen hours a day with no time off to rest, or to even spend time with God. The young missionary was just continually pushing himself, digging deep into his inner soul for strength and inspiration. He had a full schedule, in addition to preaching the Word of God every Sunday. The local villagers really loved him dearly, especially when he started building a little mission hospital as well.

On one particular Sunday morning, as was customary, the villagers came to the church for the service. However, when they arrived, the bell wasn't ringing. They didn't see the dynamic young preacher anywhere. This was most unusual, as he was always there first on a Sunday morning. The elders went to the little one-roomed grass hut where he lived to see if he was all right.

After shouting at the door and getting no response, they decided to break it down. When they got inside they were horrified at the sight that confronted them: there, lying on the floor, was the young man of God. He had killed himself. The elders walked out of that little grass hut, totally disillusioned, and went back and told the congregation. There was a great silence. The people were stunned. They walked out of the little church, closed the door behind them, and put up a sign on the door that simply said, "There is no God". Then they went back into the jungle and never returned.

> The evil one knows that if he can destroy us, then every other good thing we have done for God will amount to nothing.

What we can learn from this is that the evil one is not interested in the good works we do for Jesus; no, he's only interested in destroying us, because he knows that if he can destroy us, then every other good thing we have done for God will amount to nothing.

If there is one thing we must never sacrifice for anyone, that is our quiet time with Jesus. If we remain committed, then we shall finish this race strong for Jesus.

Devout men of God

Men of the calibre of Martin Luther and John Wesley, who impacted this world through their ministries, would never budge on compromising their quiet time with the Lord – not for anyone or anything. It is said that when Luther got really busy, he would just get up earlier in the morning to spend time with God. (Not like us who tend to have a shorter quiet time when things become very busy.) He would actually increase his precious time with the Lord.

John Wesley, they say, was once invited to visit Her Majesty, the Queen of England, at Buckingham Palace. She invited him to come and have tea with her, as she wanted to personally thank him for turning Britain from a nation of drunkards into a nation that ruled the world. He was there on time, as was his nature (a real stickler for discipline, he was), but the Queen was late. She eventually arrived with her huge entourage. With all the silver, the cutlery, the cake, and the tea set out, Wesley stood up and bowed to Her Majesty, saying he had to excuse himself, for he had another appointment. She replied that she'd only just arrived, but the man of God said that every day at a certain time he had an appointment with his King, Jesus, and with that he left the palace.

When you and I wonder why God uses some men and women to change the world, and not others, I venture to say that maybe some folk have got their priorities in order, and some haven't.

Smith Wigglesworth, the old master plumber from Yorkshire, England, was responsible for raising some twelve people or so from death by praying the prayer of faith over them. It is alleged that he was a man who never spent more than half an hour in prayer, but then again, he apparently never let half an hour go by without praying.

There are very few coincidences in life. Men and women don't move mountains for God by chance. It happens when they put God first in their lives, spend lots of time in His presence, and then step out in faith. They know Him through intimate fellowship, and the rest is a formality.

Refreshment and rejuvenation

As I am writing this book I am reminded that to have a time with the Lord in that special place, which we will call a booth, closet, or "succoth", must never ever be hard work. It must never be a chore that you feel you have to do. Rather, it should be a great joy and a pleasure – a time of refreshment, a time of rejuvenation.

My late dad, who was a blacksmith, always said to my brother and me, "If you don't feel like going to your work in the morning, change your work." Simply put, because you spend most of your time in the workplace, it should be enjoyable.

I honestly want to say that if your time with Jesus every morning is a labour of love, then it needs to stop, because then something is wrong. For me it is the opposite, for to have time with the Lord Jesus Christ every day is what keeps me alive. It is what keeps me sustained, bringing joy and vision into my life. It makes me a new man, like going away for a good holiday – a welcome break. I am always so excited to see the new revelations that the Lord is going to give me. I want to know what

> To have time with the Lord Jesus Christ every day is what keeps me alive.

He has to say to me and when I have had that time of meditation, prayer, Scripture reading, and listening to gospel music, I am ready to face whatever lies in my path.

I know some men who live the life of a martyr – they seem to think that the more they work and the less fun they have, the more holy they become. This is not the case whatsoever. If you go back to our Mentor, Jesus Christ, you will find that He continues to encourage us to have regular quiet times, just as He had with His heavenly Father. Often, when the disciples would look for Him and ask Him where He had been, He would say, "I have been with My Father".

They say a change is as good as a holiday, and I want to tell you that every day that I go into my booth is like a holiday, because I never know what God has got in store for me next.

Stepping out

As I write this book, I am preparing to go on my first ever visit to the USA. I am going to Nashville, Tennessee, via Virginia, where I will be speaking live on a huge television show. I cannot wait for that day. Obviously there is also quite a lot of apprehension of the unknown.

I wouldn't use the word "fear" – it's maybe too strong a word – but there are always a lot of things that build up inside of me before I go on a trip. As I've mentioned, one of them is that I miss my wife terribly when I am away. Even as I write this book, I'm already getting homesick. Another one is not knowing what the outcome of the trip is going to be. I just know that God wants me to go – of that I have no doubt, as He has opened so many doors.

I am very excited and I believe this is what gets me

up in the morning. It is also what chases me to my booth to spend time with God, because I know beyond any shadow of a doubt that I am not going alone. The only way that I can keep my message on the cutting edge, making it interesting and exciting, is by spending time in the presence of Almighty God. If we don't have that "time out", we will become very dull and boring to listen to, and maybe suffer from anxiety and fear.

I would really encourage you to work on that quiet time and make it as exciting as possible. Do not let anything else come between you and God at that time. We need to be in His presence. He needs our undivided attention and we need to be totally focused when we listen to Him. That is what keeps us relevant and makes our tasks in this world so very exciting.

The spice of life

They say that variety is the spice of life. I think this is especially true when having your time in the presence of God. One doesn't have to go through the same routine every day: you can read a Christian book; if you have a few hours spare, you could watch a good Christian film to broaden your outlook. Reading a good Christian magazine will also feed your spirit.

Christianity is not an organization or a club like any secular group. Christianity is a way of life and the more we understand that, the longer and more fruitful our walk with Jesus will be. This walk that I am talking about, and of having quiet time with God, is not a once-off or a seasonal thing – it is something you do until the day you go home to be with Him, where you will have a permanent quiet time with the Lord, in heaven.

It is so important to have other interests in life as a believer. For me, one of the greatest pastimes – or therapies – I have is to go horse riding on the farm. I also enjoy assisting my sons as much as I can, and just observing the wonderful things they are doing, taking the whole farming operation to the next level. That actually brings me more joy and relaxation than anything else.

"Me time"

I have to be careful, because after I have been away on a preaching tour, my wife likes to go out a bit and do things together. But for me, I'm just as happy to stay home, ride my horse, look at the cattle, observe the developments on the farm, and just be away from people and in the presence of God. That is what refreshes me and gives me hope.

Sometimes it becomes hard for me when I have been away from home for a while, sleeping in a strange bed, eating foreign food, and mingling with different people. There's nothing wrong with that, because it's my life – people are my life and God has given me a heart for the lost and those who are hurting and distressed – but there is a time when I overdo it. Then I become dull and I am "there but not there".

It's at times like this that "me time" is so important. I come home, get on my horse and go out into the veld. I speak to the Lord in raw nature, as it were. Only today I observed a cow giving birth to her calf. It's calving time on the farm right now and to see young calves and heavily pregnant mothers getting ready to calve is wonderful. It is an awesome experience to witness the birth of new life – it revitalizes me and reminds me of the basics of life.

Sometimes, my dear friend, we can become so spiritual that we are of no earthly consequence. We need to keep the balance and if we do that, we will never become dull or uninteresting, and will continue to be a joy to people who are looking for hope and for a reason to live.

Just quoting Scripture is actually not enough; people have got to see a difference in your life. For some people, you will be the only "Scripture" they ever read. If you are constantly tired and negative about everything in life, have no interest, and are boring to listen to, you have no chance of leading that person to Christ. But if you are full of vitality and can speak about practical, true-to-life issues, then you will be real to them. And if there is anything people are looking for in this day and age, it's realism. Once they see there is something totally different about you and they want what you have got, then it is just a formality when it comes to leading them to Christ. Of course, the next step is to teach them how to have fellowship on a daily basis with King Jesus.

> Just quoting Scripture is actually not enough; people have got to see a difference in your life.

Chapter 3

Time in God's Presence

The more time we spend in the presence of God, the easier it becomes to hear His still, small voice speaking to us. People have often approached me and asked how they can hear from God. They want to know how He speaks to me. Where do I get all the messages for our TV programmes, magazine articles, and books? Well, the answer is quite simple: by spending time with Jesus, every day.

I have never heard the voice of the Master audibly, and do not believe that many people have and then lived to tell the tale. Remember that when Moses came down from Mount Sinai, he had to wear a veil over his face. People could not look at him, for he had been in the presence of the very Creator of the universe. And, to boot, the Lord had only allowed Moses to see His back as He passed by.

What an incredibly powerful Creator we are talking about here! Father God was concerned that if he saw Him face to face, Moses would die. That was why, when God passed by, He hid Moses in the cleft of a rock (see Exodus 33:18–23).

I must be honest: I fear greatly for Christians who speak about the Lord with disrespect, calling Him the

"Man upstairs", or "my Buddy". They obviously have no idea whom they are speaking about. Orthodox Jews regard His name as so holy that they do not even write it down. They have the utmost reverence for Father God.

The consequences of poor hearing

How does God speak to His people in this day and age and give them instructions? Well, first and foremost, when you come into His presence to have your quiet time, you must spend a while quieting your soul in meditation and getting rid of all earthly distractions. Unless you are fully, 100 percent focused on what He has to say, the Father will definitely not give you life-changing instructions, which could have an eternal effect on your future and that of your family.

Simply put, it could even be dangerous, because if you don't hear Him clearly, it could ruin your life forever. You may not hear clearly from God because you are distracted – in a rush and thinking about the day's work ahead. You may, for example, mistakenly think that the Lord has told you to sell up, leave your job, take your young family, and move to New Zealand. You scrape all your money together and buy a one-way ticket for all of you. Thinking that you're following God's instructions, you leave, only to realize once you have arrived that it wasn't God's will for you at all; you should in fact never have left home.

I happen to love New Zealand; we had an amazing campaign there some years back, but I distinctly remember meeting people who had immigrated there from South Africa, thinking they were obeying God's instructions. They were very disappointed, to put it mildly; some actually devastated. They didn't have the money to come back home, and so have to remain there. Now this has got nothing to do with their salvation, but it means that they have to live with the consequences of their actions.

A more drastic example would be a young person who makes a decision to get married, thinking he or she has heard from God. But because they are not sitting at His feet, listening to Him, they are distracted, caught by the "love at first sight" syndrome. They make a fundamentally poor choice, like marrying an unbeliever, thinking that once they are married, they will win over their spouse for God (which hardly ever happens). They find themselves in a very hard place, not something that God cannot sort out, because nothing is too hard for Him, but stuck in a situation that will cause a lot of unnecessary pain and suffering. This could have been avoided totally by just listening to that quiet voice, saying, "This is the way..."

> When we come to have that special time with Him... don't rush God or else He will not be part of it at all.

We need to always remember that God is never, ever in a rush. He is not subject to time like we are. He created time; in fact, He is time! So when we come to have that special time with Him, preferably early in the morning, don't rush God or else He will not be part of it at all. This rushing around and busyness is not of the Lord. You know the saying: "Jesus is never early. He is never late. He is always right on time." If we start to live the way the Master meant for us to live, there would be far fewer stress-related illnesses like stomach ulcers, nervous breakdowns, depression, and so forth.

Three cups of tea

I was given a lovely little book from my daughter Robyn, called *Three Cups of Tea*. In it the author relates the story of a well-known mountaineer who was attempting to reach the summit of one of the most treacherous mountains in the Himalayas.

The mountaineer helped a friend who got into trouble during the ascent and had to bring him down from very near the top of the infamous mountain called K2. Once his friend was safe, he was too ill to return and attempt a summit. He was so weak that he lost his way through sheer exhaustion and cold, and wandered into a little village where some of the poorest people in the world live. The area was in the northernmost part of Pakistan, and the villagers took in the dying young mountaineer. They cared for him, giving all they had, and eventually he recovered. He was so grateful for their love and care that he vowed to come back and build them a school, which he subsequently did.

In nursing him back to health, these so-called primitive tribesmen taught the educated young man from the West a very serious lesson. You see, he was working his heart out trying to build the school in double-quick time, and working the builders at a tremendous pace as well. He felt that he had obligations to the donors who had given the money for the school. He was marching around with a spirit level and a plumb line, chasing everyone around.

The village elder asked the young man to go for a walk with him. He took the mountaineer away from the building site to the top of an adjoining mountain and then told him to sit down and be quiet! He asked the young man to look at the mountains, reminding him that they'd been there for thousands of years. And so, he said, have we. He told the young man, "We might be uneducated, but we are not stupid." He told the youngster he was driving them crazy!

The village elder then took the young man to his home and asked his elderly wife to make them some tea. When the tea arrived, he said to the young man that they really appreciated what he was doing for their children, but that the villagers themselves were more important than a school. He then proceeded to pour the tea, telling the young man that, traditionally, they drink three cups of tea: the first cup is given to a stranger; the second is shared with someone who is a friend; and the third when someone joins the family. And for the family, he said, the villagers would do anything – even die.

Lessons from Mary and Martha

As I read that beautiful story, I thought immediately of Mary and Martha, when Jesus came to visit them at their home in Bethany. (Can you imagine the Son of God visiting you in your home?) Well, Martha wanted everything to be just right for the Lord Jesus, so she was tearing around the place, while her sister, Mary, was sitting quietly at Jesus' feet, listening to the Son of God speak about things that no one had heard before.

Martha, if you remember, complained to Jesus and said, *"Lord, do You not care that my sister has left me to serve alone? Therefore tell her to help me"* (Luke 10:40). The Master replied, saying, *"Martha, Martha, you are worried and troubled about many things. But one thing is needed, and Mary has chosen that good part, which will not be taken away from her"* (Luke 10:41–42).

He could see that Martha was distracted and bothered about many things. If we are going to get direction from

> He won't fail us; He will give us the advice we need, no matter how big or small the issue may be.

God – instruction and godly counsel – then we are really going to have to wait upon Him. He won't fail us; He will give us the advice we need, no matter how big or small the issue may be. We will never hear consistently from God, or anyone else for that matter, if we only have five or ten minutes to spend with Him each day.

The danger of distraction

The biggest deterrent to having good, wholesome quiet times with Jesus is distraction. Please take to heart what I am saying, because, as Zig Ziglar said, "The greatest enemy of excellence is good".

The distractions from having those precious "God moments" with Jesus are not necessarily sinful things. They are often good things, like a person coming to you with a problem, needing prayer. Now any God-fearing Christian will tell you that you should help them immediately. But that is not what our Saviour did. When Lazarus was sick and his two sisters sent an urgent message to the Lord, did Jesus go straight away? The answer is a definite NO! In fact, He only arrived four days after Lazarus had been laid in the tomb. As we know, Jesus proceeded to raise Lazarus from the dead.

> Jesus was never distracted by anyone or anything; He only responded to His heavenly Father.

Jesus was never distracted by anyone or anything; He only responded to His heavenly Father. That is why His life was so effective, and why Jesus changed the world forever – in a short ministry that spanned a mere three years. If we dare to implement these godly principles in our own lives, I firmly believe we shall be used by God to move mountains for Him. After all, didn't the Master say that you and I would perform miracles even greater than those of Jesus, if we would only believe?

However, this only happens with concerted effort, through much prayer and fasting, and by spending time in His presence. Believers require extreme discipline, particularly at the beginning of their new walk of faith.

Jesus teaches us to pray

This very morning, while reading my Bible, the Father spoke to me very expressly through the book of Matthew (chapter 6; verses 5 and 8). This is where Jesus says, *"When you pray, you shall not be like the hypocrites. For they love to pray standing in the synagogues and on the corners of the streets, that they may be seen by men. Assuredly, I say to you, they have their reward… Therefore do not be like them. For your Father knows the things you have need of before you ask Him."*

> I love God's holy Word so much: It is straightforward, practical, and yet profound.

When you pray, don't babble on and on as people do sometimes. They think their prayers are answered merely by repeating their words again and again. Don't be like them. Your Father knows exactly what you need even before you ask Him!

That is why I love God's Holy Word so much: it is straightforward, practical, and yet profound. Not only does Jesus tell us where to pray and how to pray, He also shows us, practically, what to pray! Not one of us can plead ignorance and say we don't know how to pray and where to pray, or even what to pray.

In Matthew 6:9–13, Jesus teaches us to pray like this:

> *Our Father in heaven, hallowed be Your name. Your kingdom come. Your will be done on earth as it is in heaven. Give us this day our daily bread. And forgive us our debts, as we forgive our debtors. And do not lead us into temptation, but deliver us from the evil one. For Yours is the kingdom and the power and the glory forever. Amen.*

What a prayer, a complete prayer as taught to us by the Carpenter from Nazareth, Jesus! That is why I love Him so much – it's because He is for the man in the street, ordinary people like you and me. Accordingly, we need to make our quiet time with Him a priority.

Prayer in practice

Show me a man who prays a lot and I will show you a great man of God! George Müller was just such a man. He was the founder of an amazing miracle that took place in Bristol, England. By raw faith, Müller built a children's home, in which he cared for over ten thousand orphans. He established 117 schools, in which a hundred and twenty thousand children were educated. This was without making his needs known to any man, only to

God, alone in his closet.

I remember reading about an incident that took place at the orphanage late one night. The matron of one of the dormitories came to see Müller and told him, "We have enough coal for tonight, and then it is finished." Not showing any sign of anxiety, he thanked her for letting him know, and politely said it would be delivered in the morning. No sooner had she left than another woman came to say that in their dormitory, they had just fed the children their last meal – there was nothing left for breakfast. He answered as he had the first: "Don't worry, the food will be there in the morning."

> Where no one else can hear or see, God will answer.

He then went to his booth and made his requests known to God. As in the past, when he prayed the prayer of faith, God answered, and those thousands of children ate and were kept warm. The coal and food had miraculously arrived in the morning.

When he was an old man, Müller was approached by close friends who loved him dearly, saying they would like to organize a pension scheme for him so that he would have something to fall back on later. Müller, with tears of gratitude streaming down his face, said to his concerned friends that Jesus had supplied all his needs for many years and that he had never wanted for anything. He could not accept their kind offer and hurt Jesus. He thanked them and asked them to give the donation to someone else.

Müller was an incredible man of practical faith and I firmly believe that it grew and matured in his booth. We really need to start taking our needs to Jesus in our quiet time, not to the high street, where everybody can hear and see the need. I feel that our Lord would probably say, "Well, if you want your needs answered by man, then I'll just step back." Where no one else can hear or see, God will answer. Not only is He able, but, more importantly, He is completely willing! I am totally convinced that time spent in The Secret Place increases our faith in God.

God-given authority

When you call those things that are not as if they were, those huge mountains start to become mere molehills. The reason is that if you focus on Jesus, and not on the problem, those giants become grasshoppers and we become giants. When we speak, we talk with authority, not only in word, but also in the tone of our voice. Even our eyes show this God-given authority!

The eyes of a person are the windows to the heart, and that is why, when preaching, I like to look into a person's eyes. It tells you a complete story: who they are, where they have been, and, most of all, with whom they've been spending time. Remember, when Moses came down from the mountain after having spent a long time in the presence of God, he had to wear a veil over his face. The Israelites couldn't look into his face because the glory of God was evident. The Bible says that Moses' face was shining and that the Israelites could not look upon him (see Exodus 34:29–35).

When you have been in the presence of God in your booth, you become so pumped up with enthusiasm and joy. When you then open your mouth to speak, people tend to believe what you say. When they look into your eyes they see Jesus in you: positivity, confidence, peace, love. This comes about by speaking with God and spending time with Him. As the Scripture says, *"Faith comes by hearing, and hearing by the word of God"* (Romans 10:17). This cannot happen in the midst of the "madding crowd", as it were, because one very easily becomes distracted.

A word from the Lord

A few weeks ago, Dieter, one of my spiritual sons, brought me a prophetic word from God during a church service. He simply said to me that the Lord says, "Do not be distracted". It was one of the most clear words I have ever received from God. The more the Father uses us, the easier it becomes to be busy and to worry about the cares of this world, instead of focusing on Him.

Men and women who have changed the face of society, the direction of the masses, are people who spend time on their own with God. Often when they come off the platform, you will find that they are reserved by nature, some even shy and introvert. But once they get into that closet, then you see their true mettle. They feel more comfortable speaking

> Men and women who have changed the face of society are people who spend time on their own with God.

with Jesus in the quietness of their booth than they do speaking to people. Just think of John the Baptist as one example: The Master said of him, *"Among those born of women there has not risen one greater than John the Baptist"* (Matthew 11:11).

Fighting fit

When asked to pray for people to acquire more faith, I always say, "I will pray that you receive a hunger for God's Holy Word, that it will drive you to spend more time with Jesus, which will automatically enhance your faith like nothing else." There can be no doubt that quiet time enhances our faith.

During the Six-Day War, Israeli troops, suffering from fatigue from the intense fighting, would be sent back to base camp. There they would be given a hot shower and a new change of kit, and then be allowed to phone home and speak to their loved ones. They would be given a substantial meal and then sent back to the front line, fighting fit.

Now that is one of the fundamental reasons why we need to get into The Secret Place on a daily basis: to be refreshed and strengthened and, most of all, to be reassured by Father God that He has us in His care.

Our Father in heaven,

Hallowed be Your name.

Your kingdom come.

Your will be done

On earth as it is in heaven.

Give us this day our daily bread.

And forgive us our debts,

As we forgive our debtors.

And do not lead us into temptation,

But deliver us from the evil one.

For Yours is the kingdom

and the power and the glory forever.

AMEN.

Chapter 4

The Power of the Word

Often we forget what an incredible tool and weapon we have in our hands: God's Holy Word in print, the Bible. If Jesus Himself (God in the form of man) used the Word when He was tempted in the desert, then how much more should you and I do so? In fact, God says that He puts His Word above His name: *"Heaven and earth will pass away, but My words will by no means pass away"* (Mark 13:31).

If this is true, then why is it that we run around following mere men, who have a word here and a word there from God? Instead, we should go into our booth, spend time reading God's Holy Word and hearing from Him first-hand what we are to do.

People have often asked me how I read my Bible. Well, I do not for a moment say that there is a right way and a wrong way, but there is one thing we need to be very careful of, and that is opening the Bible at random and just picking a Scripture. Believing God is speaking to you in this way is very dangerous indeed. I call this "spiritual fortune telling", and that is not of God.

However, having said that, I need to reiterate that you cannot put God in a box. He will speak to us in any way He chooses. Remember, He can even use a donkey if He so desires! If you are honestly seeking answers from God, use your Bible and read it systematically. In other words, each morning go into your booth, start your quiet time with reading God's holy Bible first, and then pray afterwards.

This was how George Müller used to have his quiet time. He said that when he prayed first (before reading the Word), he would have no real thought pattern, and would end up praying haphazardly. But when he read the Bible first, the Holy Spirit would give Him direction. He would be able to pray specifically and with clarity, knowing God's heart in a particular situation.

Müller's life was evidence of this statement, because he never asked for a penny in his life. He just believed that by faith God would meet the incredible necessities that were required. And guess what? Father God met each and every need. Something like six million pounds went through Müller's hands, without Him ever having to ask for money or provisions.

Come ye apart

If you do not have a set way of reading your Bible, consider this method. You don't have to read it consecutively from Genesis to Revelation, but read each book from beginning to end, say ten to fifteen verses each day. As I've said, reading it in the first person makes it more personal and real. Have your notebook at hand and write down what you believe God is telling you through those specific Scriptures.

> Have your notebook at hand and write down what you believe God is telling you.

God's holy Bible must be the cornerstone of time spent in His presence. That is why, to be honest, I cannot believe a person can have a proper quiet time without the Bible. Some say their quiet time consists of going for a long walk in the veld, or along a beautiful stretch of sandy beach beside the ocean, the wind blowing through their hair while they admire God's beautiful creation. Doing this is just great. It is invigorating and I often do it myself on the farm – admiring the cattle and their calves, the beautiful horses, the sunrises and sunsets. However, this is not having a quiet time before God. It's a wonderful time of meditation and reflection, of thanking the Father for His creation, but it's not taking time out to hear the still voice of God.

I once read a book by the well-known author Philip Yancey, who spoke of a young woman who had won the Pulitzer Prize for writing. He described the place where she wrote: down in the basement under the house, with one solitary light, a table and chair, and four roughly finished, unplastered walls. That was it. An exciting event for her was changing a blue pen for a black one. What is the point I am making? It is this: when we want to get into the presence of God, and we really want to hear from Him, we must not be distracted at all.

> When we want to get into the presence of God... we must not be distracted at all.

We need to hear from God through His Holy Word. Therefore the Bible must be our total focus at that time and nothing else – not the clouds blowing across the sky, not the waves crashing onto the sandy beaches, not the beautiful horses racing through the green fields, but God and God alone.

Whenever Jesus calls me to make a major decision in my life, my family, or even in the ministry, He always confirms it through Scripture.

First love

To give you a practical example, in 2003 my wife, Jill, and I went to the Mkhuze Game Reserve for a rest. We love the bush and wildlife, which we find very therapeutic. It had been an extremely busy time, and we needed a complete break. Early one morning I was sitting in the presence of God, just listening to the voice of Africa. As I drank my tea, I could hear baboons calling to each other, and the mighty African Fish Eagle, circling high up and making that unmistakable call.

I thanked God for many things: for being alive, for my beautiful family, for the Christian work He had called me to do. So many amazing doors had been opened for me to preach the gospel, and we had booked trips to India and Newfoundland, and other places that were new to me. I drained the last few drops of tea and opened my beloved Bible. At that time I was reading the book of Revelation, and I continued from where I had left off the previous day.

What I read shocked me to the core. The Lord spoke almost audibly to me: "*Nevertheless I have this against you, that you have left your first love. Remember therefore from where you have fallen; repent and do the first works, or else I will come to you quickly and remove your lampstand from its place*" (Revelation 2:4–5).

Let me digress for a moment. We are all familiar with nightmares: a huge, vicious, man-eating lion running towards you, or someone chasing you. Just as the lion pounces or the stranger catches you, you wake up in a cold sweat. Now for me a nightmare is walking onto a platform to preach the Word of God at a sports stadium full of people, without the Holy Spirit. It is something I would not wish on my worst enemy.

Basically what Jesus was saying to me was, "Go home and get back to your first love: spending time with Me, like you did when you were a new Christian." We can often get so busy doing the work of the Lord that we neglect the Lord of the work, and that is what He was saying to me very clearly!

Well, back home the first thing I did was cancel all my preaching engagements for the year. That is not an easy thing to do, since one can become very unpopular, especially when your hosts have been preparing for at least a year in advance. But the Bible says obedience is better than sacrifice, and the first miracle happened: I received very few complaints. The organizers simply said that if God had told me to cancel, then who are they to argue with God?

Confirmation from the Word

I called upon the name of the Lord and asked, "What am I to do with the rest of my life now?" I felt the Lord say, "I want you to mentor young men, for there are very few spiritual fathers in these days." Thinking He meant maybe three or four young men, what an amazing surprise I was soon to get, with the birth of the Mighty Men™ phenomenon sweeping the world!

> Remember, a good idea does not always equate to a God idea.

We need to really consider confirmation from God's Holy Word before making any decisions or changes. Remember, a good idea does not always equate to a God idea, and furthermore a need does not justify a call. Jesus never healed all those who were sick when He was on earth, and He never fed all the hungry people either. He only did what His heavenly Father told Him to do.

What is so very reassuring when you step out of the boat and walk on water for Jesus is that when you have had a clear word from God and the huge mountains come along (and they will), you can take hold of the promises God gave you through the Scriptures. They will be a tremendous source of strength. One thing I have experienced to be so true in my walk with the Lord is that the Word of God will never, ever return void. His Word is "yea", and "amen"!

God's promises

It is good practice to memorize the precious Scriptures that God gives you, so that you can, with the greatest love and respect, remind the Master of His promises. That is exactly what Moses did in the wilderness when God was angry with the children of Israel. He was going to destroy the whole nation, but Moses reminded Him of His promises. The Bible tells us that God relented, which literally means He changed His mind (see Exodus 23:8–14). God puts His Holy Word before His name.

That is why I love God so much – to think that our Creator would humble Himself, and take counsel from His own creation. It's really amazing! When your little

> What an incredibly gracious God we serve.

son or daughter wants to give you advice, you normally feel like saying to them, "I was doing these things before you were even born!" But you don't say that; you take their counsel lovingly, and implement it wholeheartedly. That's what God did. What an incredibly gracious God we serve.

Recently I was meditating on what the Word of God really represents, what it stands for. Well, it is actually Jesus Christ in print.

If a curious person had to ask you the question, "This Saviour of yours, where can I meet Him?" how would you answer? Well, in the last book of the Bible, the book of Revelation, Jesus is called "The Word of God" (Revelation 19:13). That is why time in The Secret Place every day is so vital.

If you need to make decisions or seek counsel about literally anything, it's available to you at no charge. No appointment is necessary and it is totally confidential.

It's the "Word" that created heaven and earth, and His name is Jesus Christ.

The other morning while reading a daily devotional, the writer was saying that the greatest asset for anyone is to know that Jesus walks with us every day, and He never, ever leaves us or forsakes us. But to really *know* this is a great asset indeed. Some of us tend to know this fact in our heads, but we need to get to know it in our spiritual person too.

There is a story about Martin Luther, the great reformer. He was seen sitting at a wooden table during a difficult time of testing, writing over and over again on the table, the words "He lives, He lives".

Spending time in the Word of God every morning will remind us during the day that Jesus is walking right alongside us. We have nothing to fear, for *"If God is for us, who can be against us?"* (Romans 8:31). Of course, the answer is no one.

Chapter 5

A Place of Comfort

The room or location for our quiet time should be a place of shelter from the storms of life, a place of comfort when we are hurting, fearful, or disappointed.

One of the darkest moments in my life was when I lost my little nephew through a tractor accident on our farm, Shalom. That was about twenty-five years ago, and yet I remember it like yesterday. If it were not for the fact that I was having regular times with Jesus in my booth, I can honestly tell you that I would not be writing this book. I would probably be in a mental home, or in the gutter, or a hopeless drug addict or alcoholic. Everyone needs to have a place where they can go, a place where they can get away from the extreme pressures of this hectic life.

> It is vital that we have a real and living experience with Jesus Christ, because we have no idea what tomorrow holds in store.

It is vital that we have a real and living experience with Jesus Christ, because we have no idea what tomorrow holds in store for us. On that particular day, we were celebrating Jill's birthday and my brother,

Fergus, and his family had come from Johannesburg to spend a short holiday with us. The children were all playing cricket on the lawn in the front of our little house – Fergus is a professional sportsman and so he was busy teaching them. The rest of us were working, and I had just come in to have a quick cup of tea with everyone.

Just then there was a knock at the door. It was our tractor driver, saying his tractor was stuck and asking if I could please come with another one to pull him out. Naturally, I said it was no problem and that I'd be along shortly. I shouted to the family that I'd be back soon and walked out of the back door up towards the shed where the other tractor was parked.

Painful memories

As I walked up the garden path, I felt a little hand slip into mine. It was my little four-year-old nephew, Alistair, asking me where I was going. (I was his favourite uncle and he loved John Deere tractors.) I told him I was going to get a tractor to help pull out another one that was stuck in the mud. He asked if he could come along and I replied, "If your daddy says it's all right, then you can come with."

> I jumped off the tractor and picked up the limp little body. Alistair died right there in my arms.

His dad said it was fine and so off we set, me driving and Alistair standing on the running board on my right. His sister, Kirsty, stood on my left, with the tractor driver standing on the tow hitch at the back. Everybody was happy; it was a beautiful morning and the sun was shining as we drove slowly up the road.

At a slight bend in the road, I eased off on the accelerator, and the next thing little Ali fell forward off the tractor, going straight under the huge rear wheel. His sister screamed. I slammed on the brakes, but it was too late – that little blond-haired boy, the apple of his mother's eye, was lying in the middle of the road in a pool of blood. Crying out to God for help, I jumped off the tractor and picked up the limp little body. Alistair died right there in my arms.

At that moment a neighbour came along in his vehicle. We drove to the hospital in town, me holding Alistair in my arms, where the doctor officially pronounced him dead. It was without doubt the single biggest shock I've ever had in my life, an experience I would not wish on anybody. It's something you never really get over.

My brother, two-and-a-half years younger than me, walked up the steps at the entrance of the hospital, his young wife, Joanne, at his side. His hands were outstretched, and he asked, "Angus? My son?" and I had to tell him, "Your son is with Jesus, Fergie." They both broke down, weeping uncontrollably. All I could say was, "I am so very sorry." Never again do I wish to walk that hellish road. Even writing this account so many years later is still very painful for me.

Our family was so supportive during the ensuing days and months, especially my brother and sister-in-law, though they also had their own huge burden of grief to deal with. Jill was like an angel, reminding me that it was an accident, that I shouldn't blame myself. I'll never forget Lindi, my eldest daughter, running into the house when she first heard about it, throwing her arms around my neck and saying, "Dad, it's not your fault." There was such incredible love and support from our neighbours, and friends from town. Many phoned and sent their condolences, some not even knowing what to say, just breaking down and weeping with me.

For days afterwards I couldn't eat, and I battled to fall asleep at night. Jill would try to stay awake with me for as long as she could, but eventually she would collapse into a deep sleep from total exhaustion. It was a terribly emotional time for us all.

A place of comfort

This is where the "place of comfort" comes in. My alarm clock is always set for four o'clock every morning and, as is my custom, I pray with Jill. We pray for the family and then I go and make tea. I go up to my Secret Place and spend not only quality time with Jesus, but also quantity time as well.

In those early days after the terrible accident, I would lie in bed, awake, just waiting to hear the alarm go off. I'd go straight to my booth and wait to hear life-giving instructions from the Lord. Not once was I ever disappointed. It was like manna from heaven every single morning: fresh, nourishing, and life-giving. Just like the Father used the ravens to feed Elijah when he was at his lowest, Jesus fed me, and slowly but surely every day I got stronger.

It was God's Holy Word that ultimately did it for me. I would open my Bible and the Scripture would shout out to me from the page, verses

> I really want to encourage you to take God's holy Word as your comfort.

like "*Be strong in the Lord and in the power of His might*" (Ephesians 6:10). Then I would read a little further, and Jesus would say, "*Stand therefore*" (verse 14). I'd go out and allow the Lord to fight the good fight for me, and by faith I would remain standing.

That is basically how I have got through many times of hardship in my life, and I really want to encourage you to take God's Holy Word as your comfort. Let your booth be a place of consolation and reassurance when you face huge tests. There are certain trials in our lives that we will never get over, but I can testify that as time moves on, those tidal waves start becoming smaller, and the pain less sharp. Father God, through His Word, soothes our wounds and heals them.

We become better people for these trials and tribulations. In fact, I have never met a man or woman worth their salt who has not been through fiery tests in life; it is unfortunately the only thing that builds character. Show me a person who has never been through difficulties and I will show you a person who has got nothing to say, has no convictions, and is not prepared to stand up for righteousness and truth.

Some of the closest encounters I have ever had with God were during my darkest days, when the storm was at its absolute worst. He was there, telling me (almost audibly) that He would never leave me or forsake me.

As a farmer I can tell you that the darker the clouds, the more life-giving the rain that those clouds carry. So never be afraid of what the future holds in store for you. As long as you are spending time in your booth with Jesus every day, you *will* be able to cope with anything that comes across your path. God did say that He would never allow us to be tempted beyond that which we can handle, and that He would always provide us with a way of escape.

Chapter 6

Faithfulness

There is one thing that is important to understand and it is this: if we intend to have close fellowship with our Lord, we need to be consistent in our quiet times with Him. We need to be faithful – not compromising our precious time with Jesus and using it for doing other things or thinking about them, as "good" as they might be. The Lord requires our total and undivided attention.

I have learned something very important during my journey with God – that He is a jealous God, and He will not share His time with you with anyone or anything else. Jesus really covets His time with us; indeed, He requires our full attention when we have fellowship with Him.

Faithful friends

One of the most faithful animals on earth has to be our canine companion, the dog. It is for good reason that he is referred to as man's best friend. No matter how people treat their dog, he remains so faithful.

I really have to control myself when I see a man kicking his faithful little dog, all because he had a hard day at the office and it didn't go well for him. These special creatures are so forgiving. The dog may suffer abuse, but he just wags his tail, as if to say, "I don't know what that was for, but I love you anyway."

We have a very special children's home on the farm, where twenty-seven children live, ranging in age from two years to twenty-three. Each one is so special to us. The children live in cottages, six per cottage, with a resident house mother in each. We also have a chaplain, an administrator, and a visiting medic. Jill is the mother of the home, and I am "Dad" whenever I am there.

But the real characters are two little dogs, cross-breeds that ended up at the home by default. One is called Rubus and the other is Rusty. These two little dogs love our children with such passion and commitment that it brings tears to one's eyes. The children almost seem to take them for granted, and yet the dogs are very protective, especially when there are visitors.

> These two little dogs love our children with such passion and commitment.

On one occasion, Jill returned to the home quite late after spending the day in town organizing clothes for the new school year. They had left early in the morning in our big bus to go to the neighbouring town. Everyone, from the youngest to the oldest, including the house mothers, went along. No one was left behind. As Jill drove back later that afternoon, there were the two faithful little dogs, lying at the entrance. They never moved from their station all day, not even leaving for a drink of water or something to eat. Rubus and Rusty waited faithfully all day until the bus came home with their loved ones. The two dogs were overwhelmed, so joyful to see the children and grateful that their friends had returned safely.

Rubus is quite a character and causes lots of trouble on Sunday mornings during the church service. The chapel is about a kilometre and a half from the home, and the children walk there together. Rubus will not stay at home and insists on following the gang to church! This causes a lot of distractions during the actual service, as the little dog runs underneath the chairs and up and down the rows looking for the children. Needless to say, Rubus always finds them.

One Sunday morning he was causing quite a disturbance, and our pastor decided enough was enough. He tackled Rubus in the middle of the service, and got quite badly bitten for his troubles. Since then it is the duty of one of the older children to lock Rubus up at the home before going to church. But somehow that dog seems to find his way out and he lands up in the middle of the congregation again. He lies underneath the children's chairs, making them all thoroughly embarrassed, but it doesn't seem to worry Rubus in the slightest. He is content as long as he is with his beloved children. And it doesn't seem to bother the pastor anymore – he and Rubus have made peace and he doesn't try to remove the dog anymore.

> That is the kind of love and dedication I believe the Master is looking for from you and me.

On a serious note, that is the kind of love and dedication I believe the Master is looking for from you and me. He wants a steadfast, immovable, and reliable love, with no fear of man, desiring only to be in close fellowship with Him. There are no strings attached and nothing is requested in return, because we love to be in His presence and that is a reward in itself.

Sometimes it takes two little dogs living at a small country children's home to teach us valuable lessons about life. Rubus and Rusty get no special attention but have adopted those little children as their own. They do not expect anything in return, save just being allowed to be in their company. That is what we call genuine, unconditional love. In our early morning quiet times, that is what Jesus wants from you and me: to meet Him because He's been waiting for us.

A dog's tale

Talking about the issue of waiting, did you ever read or hear about the true story of the dog that waited for his master for many years? Several movies have been made about the dog, but the original events took place in Japan. The dog's name was Hachikó ("*hachi*" meaning "eight", a number referring to the dog's birth order in the litter, and "*kó*" meaning "prince" or "duke").

Hachikó, a purebred Akita, is remembered for his remarkable loyalty, even many years after his death in 1935. Every day Hachikó would wait at the Shibuya train station for his owner, Professor Ueno, to return from Tokyo University and they would walk home together. One day Ueno passed away unexpectedly at work, but that did not stop Hachikó. He returned to the train station every day, appearing at the time the train was due at the station. He waited patiently for his master for nine years, earning the title of "*chóken Hachikó*" ("faithful dog Hachikó"). Several articles were published about him and he became a national sensation, with commuters bringing him treats to help him in his wait. A bronze statue of him was erected at the Shibuya tation, known as the "Hachikó entrance exit", and bronze pawprints mark the exact location where he waited for his master for all those years.

Isn't it amazing how the world respects faithfulness, even in a humble dog? When you hear of couples celebrating fifty years together, it becomes an enormous talking point and sometimes you'll find an article about them in the newspaper. I believe it's because faithfulness is such a rare quality these days where everyone is rushing around. People are always in a hurry and they never seem to have the time to sit down and have a chat with one another.

Well, Jesus is never in a rush. He remains waiting patiently to speak to you and me every day. Do you know of another person busier than the Creator of this entire universe? Yet He makes time for you and me, because He genuinely loves us so much. Remember, He does not need us, but He badly wants to know us. That is the reason He created us – for fellowship, nothing else. I firmly believe that our Master gets lonely, and just wants us to have fellowship with Him. We need to become much more faithful towards God, and show up regularly each morning in our little booth. He will be there without fail, waiting for us, never late. What a mighty, intimate Father we serve.

Chapter 7

The Mental Booth

When one travels a lot, it is very hard to have a consistent quiet time. Our Lord Jesus has shown me a special way to come away from the crowds, and have a special, intimate time with Him. At this point I need to make it very clear that I am in no way speaking about positive thoughts; I am purely making a place in my heart where I can have undivided fellowship with Jesus.

Let me draw you a picture. Imagine you are sitting in an international airport on the other side of the world. You are dead tired, what with jet lag and the proverbial hurry-up-and-wait syndrome. Your connecting flight has been delayed for three hours and you are miles from home. Another preaching campaign lies ahead, which will last for another few days. Only then will you be homeward bound. You are homesick and your emotional tank is on reserve. At the last church where you preached, you gave it your all and, to top it off, you are feeling very lonely.

This is what God has given to me, and I sincerely hope it will help you too: I like to check in as early as possible at the airport and then go straight through to the departure lounge. I find out when my plane is due to leave, find the departure gate number, then walk through and find a comfortable seat right opposite the boarding gate.

I put my boarding pass in my pocket and check my watch to see how much time I have before we are called to board. I close my eyes, tuning out the noise of an international airport – different flight numbers being called, people boarding, aeroplanes coming in to land and taking off.

The place in my mind

There is a place in my mind where I go; yes, a mental booth, which I'd like to describe to you. It's a place in the Luapula Province, up in the northern part of Zambia. It's very close to the Congo, where David Livingstone was laid to rest. There is a long path right in the middle of the tropical rain forest, and it is very quiet. There is only the sound of wild birds chattering away to each other. These beautiful tall, indigenous trees almost join at the top, like a green cathedral. If you walk along this path for a few hundred metres, you'll find an old log lying by the side of the path. In my imagination, I stop there and take a seat. Just in front of me is a beautiful wetland, winding its way down the valley. A gentle breeze rises up, just what a person needs to combat the intense heat.

> In this place in my mind I quietly have a heart-to-heart talk with the Lover of my soul.

In this place in my mind I quietly have a heart-to-heart talk with the Lover of my soul. It's not a shopping list that I speak about, like my elderly friends give me. No, it is anything but. It's a discussion that one would have with an intimate friend, telling them about how you are feeling.

I tell Jesus that I am tired and missing my wife; that I'm concerned about how the children are doing; about not knowing what to speak about at the next campaign. I tell Him I'm hoping not to let my hosts down, because they spent so much on my airfare and on organizing the event. My thoughts return home and I tell the Lord that I'm feeling a bit uneasy about Jill being on the farm at night all by herself with the children, with no security guard. I pray that the cattle and sheep will be safe.

Slow down, Angus!

It's normally at about this point in my talk with Jesus that I feel Him say, "Whoa, Angus. Just calm down and listen for a moment. I can hear that you are very tired. First of all, Jill is just fine. Remember, I promised you both that I would never leave you or forsake you. And besides, Bhengu, your big, strong foreman, told you clearly that you must go and preach My Word. He promised to look after your wife and children, and to care for the livestock on the farm. With regard to your message at the next appointment, what are you concerned about? Don't I normally give you the words of life to speak anyway? Don't worry about anything; I have everything under complete control, in the very palm of My hand."

Then there is a calm that starts to descend upon me, like a gentle, misty, cool rain. It puts my troubled soul immediately at peace. It refreshes me in a way I cannot explain. I thank my blessed Lord for His infinite

> There is a calm that starts to descend upon me... It puts my troubled soul immediately at peace.

goodness towards me and my loved ones, and then I hear the announcement that my flight is about to board. I'm back in the present and it's time for the passengers to present their boarding passes to the attendant at the gate. I stand up, have a good long stretch as if I've had a long, restful sleep, and, totally refreshed, board the plane for my next destination.

You see, Father God says in His Holy Word, *"Call to Me, and I will answer you, and show you great and mighty things, which you do not know"* (Jeremiah 33:3) and that is exactly what happens every time I go into my mental "postinia" – my mental booth. Jesus speaks to me; He reassures me and directs me and, most of all, He reminds me just how much He loves me!

Chapter 8

Increased Faith

If we desire to walk by faith, and not by sight, then we desire a very good and honourable thing, but it will never happen if we are not spending quality time in God's presence. We know only too well what the Word of God says about obtaining faith: *"Faith comes by hearing, and hearing by the word of God"* (Romans 10:17).

What I have experienced in my own life, and have read much about in the lives of the saints who have gone before us, is that all of them, without exception, spent time in The Secret Place with their blessed Saviour, Jesus Christ. This includes people like Martin Luther, John Wesley, Dwight L. Moody, Amy Carmichael, Mary Slessor, Charles H. Spurgeon, Andrew Murray, William Booth, and Billy Graham, to mention but a few.

> The more time they spent with Jesus, the more their faith increased.

How does one come to this conclusion? Well, you see, when we get out of the boat and walk on the stormy seas of life, often the waves become so huge that we cannot see land. Then we had better know this miracle-working God, because if we don't, we are surely going to drown! These men and women of God found that the more time they spent with Jesus, the more their faith increased, and the smaller their challenges became. This was simply because they didn't focus on their problems but rather on the problem-solver, Jesus Christ. When we spend more time in the world, looking at our challenges through secular eyes, the challenges seem to become bigger, until they simply overwhelm us.

As we have our quiet time with the Lord and focus on the signs, wonders, and miracles He performed, then we start to believe that all things *are* possible for those who believe (see Mark 9:23). This makes us realize that this life has little to do with flesh and blood. It actually involves principalities and powers of the air. It is a spiritual battle that we are involved in, not a fight against flesh and blood. If we aren't standing in faith, then we start to weaken at the knees.

Jesus, the problem-solver

I remember a huge challenge I was faced with during the preparation of the 2009 Mighty Men™ Conference. Only a couple of days before the conference was due to start, Jill and I went for a run early in the morning. The weather had turned and it started raining. It became so cold that the rain was turning into sleet, and we thought it might snow. Now these men who were about to arrive were going to camp out in the open, many thousands of them; some for a week, others for three or four days. They were arriving from all over South Africa and other parts of the world. We worried about the massive sound system, as it could not take moisture in the speakers.

As the two of us ran side by side, the weather seemed to become worse. I could hear the devil whispering,

"The big coaches are going to get stuck in the mud; the men will all leave as it will be far too cold; the hay bales (seating) will be wet..." and so on. My spirit was starting to become very fearful!

I couldn't wait to get back home with Jill, into a hot shower, and then run for The Secret Place, reminding myself of the promises God gave me about my role in mentoring young people. He promised He would do it, and He did.

What an incredible Holy Spirit happening that conference turned out to be. And of course the weather turned around the day before the conference started. It was beautiful and temperate. The men came in their droves, more than we had ever dreamt of, and we had an enormous harvest. Yes, God is very good!

Chapter 9

Preparation

I received the following quotation from one of my dear spiritual sons: "Give me six hours to chop down a tree, and I will spend the first four sharpening the axe" (Abraham Lincoln). Of course, the moral of the quote is: Don't lose your cutting edge!

This made me reflect on how important it is for men and women to have a booth to go to. This is particularly important for those who have huge responsibilities in society, in order for them to be able to make the correct decisions in life. Those decisions could very well affect an entire nation!

Apart from being a strong believer, Lincoln was an extremely practical man. You can tell from his remarks that he was a deep thinker, and that's what Jesus wants from you and me. Once, while in the White House, Lincoln looked out of the oval room window and made a comment, saying that the street sweeper he could see would never amount to anything.

Lincoln's senators were quite shocked at the president's statement. After all, he always stood up for the poor and oppressed (and was instrumental in the abolition of the slave trade in the USA). Respectfully, they asked Lincoln how he could make such a judgment about a poor street sweeper. He told them to look for themselves – the man was sweeping the leaves against the wind.

None of us can say we are busier than the president of the USA. Accordingly, we need to spend a lot more time in The Secret Place in preparation. We will find that the Holy Spirit will give us wisdom to make good decisions, become more observant, and be sharper in the market place. This is important even in the day-to-day issues, where we are required to make so-called mundane choices.

Make a point to come aside

Just the other day while reading the Bible Jesus spoke very clearly to me in the Gospel of Mark. In chapter 9, Jesus takes His disciples aside because He wants to teach them (see Mark 9:30–31). Jesus tries to keep His whereabouts as secret as possible and so He takes only His disciples with Him. The Lord shows very clearly that it is important to "come aside". This is especially difficult for us in a world where so much is happening, where our iPod®, iPad®, and cell phone keeps us continually in contact with others without any effort at all. It is very hard for a committed Christian to be on their own.

> The Lord shows very clearly that it is important to "come aside".

When I first came to Shalom some thirty-five years ago, we had no telephone. In those days there were no cell phones and we had no contact with the outside world until we got our little wind-up telephone. Because the farm we had purchased was literally in the bush, there was no infrastructure or telephone poles. We couldn't even see our neighbours because we built our house in an overgrown forest. Accordingly, being on one's own was not difficult at all. We had to drive to town to find company or to meet people and socialize. Now, however, the pendulum has swung completely. In fact, to have a semblance of privacy, my family has had to put up an electric gate at the entrance to our farm.

I would like to address any believers who think that because they've given their lives to the Lord, their lives are no longer their own but God's. Well, that's quite true because in Galatians Paul . says: "*I have been crucified with Christ; it is no longer I who live, but Christ lives in me*" (Galatians 2:20). However, having said that, we do need to have that intimate quiet time with the Lord ourselves and obviously with our immediate family. And that needs to be worked on. We do need to do it, because people can be very persuasive. It is never intentional, but people tend to think that their particular problem is the most important problem in the world – that is just human nature.

> We do need to have that intimate quiet time with the Lord ourselves and obviously with our immediate family.

I remember very distinctly once when I was sick (something that happens very rarely), I had a serious case of the flu and was in bed. The phone rang and a man said he had to speak to me urgently. He insisted on speaking to me, and my wife was trying to tell him that I wasn't well and not able to come to the telephone. She asked him to call in a couple of days' time, but he would have none of it, insisting that he had to speak to me immediately.

At that moment my young son came through the kitchen door. The phone was right in the kitchen and he overheard a part of the conversation. He literally took the phone from his mother and said, "Maybe you didn't hear my mum clearly, but my dad is not well and won't come to the phone." The man replied that if he didn't speak to me, he was going to take his life. My son, whether rightly or wrongly, said, "Sir, you better do what you have to do, but you are still not speaking to my dad." The man didn't take his life, but he was very manipulative and insistent. I think many people may have said similar things to the Master when He was on earth, but the Lord was never influenced by human opinion one way or another. He did only what His Father told Him to do. If you look through the four Gospels, you will find that many a time when the disciples were looking for Jesus, He was spending time with His Father. Everyone was literally standing still, waiting to hear from God through Jesus, yet He did not allow the pressure to get to Him

I firmly believe that many people who suffer from mood disorders, anxiety, and so forth have actually worn themselves out, to the point where they have nothing left to give. Many of them are wonderful people and they have literally spent themselves giving to others. The sad part about life is that the person who insisted on speaking to them in the first place would simply go and find somebody else if they were turned away.

Taking the initiative

We really need to take time out to spend with God. If we don't, nobody else will, so we need to take the initiative. We need to lay down the law and insist on spending time with God. We will find ourselves refreshed and, more than anything else, we will have something to offer others. If we don't do this, the very same people who insist on taking up our time and eventually get their own way, will find that we are exhausted and cannot give them good, godly counsel. They will still blame us and be disappointed, yet off they will go to find somebody else. It is therefore in our best interests to come aside and be quiet for a time.

> It is therefore in our best interests to come aside and be quiet for a time.

They tell me that when the French Revolution took place and the Republic of France was formed, instead of having six days' work and resting on the seventh, they decided to do everything in tens. They would work for ten days and then have a day off, but it didn't work because the horses were literally falling down in the streets and collapsing because they were totally exhausted. Now if that is what happens to God's creation – the animals – then how much more is it relevant to us? Even God Himself took one day off to rest – the Sabbath.

For six days the Lord made heaven and earth and on the seventh day He rested (see Genesis 2:1–3), and there is a good reason for that. It is not just physical rest that we need, it is mental and spiritual rest too. And yet when I look around me in this day and age I am very disturbed when I see on the Sabbath day that everybody goes shopping, working mothers try to do their washing and housekeeping... when do they rest? That is why many people end up using drugs, tranquillisers or something else to stimulate them so that they can keep going. Eventually it stops working and they end up in a heap on the ground, just totally worn out.

A calm attitude

We were never made to be like this. Yes, we were created to work, something that should be enjoyable and good fun. I am enjoying my life at the moment more than I ever have before, yet I am working harder than I have ever worked. However, I am in constant fellowship with the King of kings and the Lord of lords.

We need to take that time out. What's the old saying? "All work and no play, makes Jack a dull boy."

A special word to those who are aspiring preachers: you need information, you need stories, and you need examples to tell people – otherwise you will become a boring preacher. You also need to take time out to rest. I read a beautiful example of this in the life of Sir Francis Drake, a great hero and one of England's father figures. The French army was advancing towards the shores of England. At the time, the English had the most powerful navy in the world. Drake was having a game of bolts when he saw the French army approaching the white cliffs of Dover. Instead of panicking or rushing to his ship, he finished his game of bolts first and then proceeded to do battle. Unsurprisingly, he won the day.

When we have a calm attitude we can think carefully and plan properly and then we will be successful. But when we are living a life of continuous disaster- and crisis management, we cannot sustain that kind of lifestyle. We need to draw back.

As a brand-new Christian, I would have preached anywhere and everywhere that I could, but I received very few invitations. I think the Lord orchestrated that because He knew it was all about Angus Buchan in those days and not about Jesus. Since then, as I have grown older and matured, I receive numerous, very tempting invitations to speak at large gatherings, yet I seem to spend my life saying, "Sorry, I can't make it." The reason is because I need to spend time with God; otherwise I will have nothing to offer. It seems that when God can trust us to spend time with Him, then He opens doors for us. But until that time, He will be reluctant to give us those invitations. Remember, at the end of the day, it's all about the Lord, not about you or me.

> I need to spend time with God; otherwise I will have nothing to offer.

Yes, indeed, we need to come aside and give the Lord time to speak into our lives.

Chapter 10

Home Time

I have just finished Billy Graham's latest book, called *Nearing Home*, which really touched my heart very deeply. Graham is over ninety years old now and this book was written from the heart, very challenging indeed. He says that all his life he was taught how to die as a Christian, but no one ever taught him how he ought to live in the years before he died. As we know, "growing old ain't for sissies".

Graham says in his book that he is looking forward to "home time", to heaven. He misses his wife, his best friend for almost sixty-four years. With old age comes all the elements and physical disabilities that make it tough. But old age does not disqualify us from being significant in life – finishing well is the most important attribute of a mighty man or woman of God. As you know yourself, in many sports, it's not the one who starts well who is the hero, but the one who finishes first.

> Old age does not disqualify us from being significant in life.

If we look around us today we see that the world is full of fatherless children. There is an acute shortage of grandfathers – especially godly and wise grandfathers.

Often when a man gets to pension age he literally gives up. He goes to the "waiting room" and he waits to die. I hope that I will never be one of those sitting in the waiting room and waiting to die. I can honestly say to you that I am living life to the full at the moment; in fact, I'm busier and have more purpose for living than I ever did as a young man before I met Jesus Christ.

Wisdom comes from God

You see, wisdom does not come from learning – wisdom comes from God. And the more time you spend with God, the wiser you become, because the more of God is deposited into you. That is why you will find that older men and women are not so quick to criticize others. They move much slower, not because their bodies are getting frail, but because they have learnt from the hard knocks that life has dealt them to take their time and to count the cost before they commit themselves to anything. They are no longer as impulsive as they used to be when they were young. The hardships of life teach a person to be more patient and more understanding.

You may find also that older people are less judgmental than those who are young; for them, it's not a case of black and white – there is more to it than that. When a young person would just condemn somebody out of hand, an older person may say, "No, there must be another side to the story." For example, a young person would probably write off a drunk sitting on the pavement with a bottle of alcohol, but the older person would say something like, "I wonder if that man had to go to war. You'll probably find that he is battling to come to grips with things that he saw or went through. Or maybe he lost a loved one and cannot reconcile himself with it, and instead is drowning his sorrows." There are always reasons for things and it is just too easy to write people off. As you get older, you start to realize this.

Graham says that God has a reason for keeping us here in old age. If He didn't, He would have taken us home to heaven far sooner.

Cherish the Bible now

One of my favourite photographs is of an old gentleman sitting in his rocking chair outside his log cabin reading his Bible. And that is synonymous to me for having a quiet time. It is no good waiting until you are old and aged and then learning to appreciate, love, understand, and cherish the Word of God. You have got to start reading it from a young age. At the moment I have sitting on my desk in my quiet time room three different versions of the Bible. I have the King James Version, the New King James Version and the New Living Translation.

> I love to go through the Bible and compare the different translations.

I also have a number of other versions in my book case an arm's length away. The reason is because I love to go through the Bible and compare the different translations.

The Word of God becomes life to me. After all, Jesus said that He came to give us abundant life (see John 10:10) and I don't think it's just about being physically fit. I think it's also about being spiritually healthy, and that comes from years and years of hard training. Once again Graham says in *Nearing Home* that the best way to meet the challenges of old age is to prepare for them when you are younger – before you actually arrive. There is only one way to do that and that is by learning to have a consistent quiet time with God every day.

Our Helper and Comforter

When you are young and wild and foolish, you feel like you can take on the world single-handedly. Well, that's how I felt anyway, but as you grow older you realize that this is not actually possible – you can't do everything on your own. You need God's guidance, His strength, His continued support, and you learn to lean on Him, which is actually what He wants. That is why He says in Matthew 11, *"Come to Me, all you who labor and are heavy laden, and I will give you rest"* (Matthew 11:28). The sooner we realize this, the better.

The Holy Spirit is known as the Helper and Comforter. Jesus said, *"Nevertheless I tell you the truth. It is to your advantage that I go away; for if I do not go away, the Helper will not come to you; but if I depart, I will send Him to you"* (John 16:7).

Even though I was baptized in the Holy Spirit just after I gave my life to Christ in 1979, I feel that I have not given Him enough

> The Holy Spirit is a true Friend that sticks closer than a brother.

place in my life, and of course that has been to my own detriment. He has been with me always. When you give your life to Jesus Christ, the Holy Spirit comes into your life, but when you get baptized in the Holy Spirit, you get enveloped by Him. The outward signs are not just receiving a new language, which is very precious, but the power that goes with it.

If we remember, Peter, who was an absolute coward when it came to standing up for the Lord, was asked three times whether he was one of the Galileans who followed Jesus. Peter denied it vehemently, saying he had nothing to do with this man Jesus (see Luke 22:54–62). Peter ran away like a rat in a slum.

So what happened to Peter? He got baptized by the Holy Spirit in the Upper Room. After that, Peter went out into the public places in Jerusalem and preached the gospel. No fewer than three thousand souls were added to the church as a result. This is a practical example of what happens when you embrace the Holy Spirit. To me, He is even more than just a tremendous source of strength and power; He is a Friend, a true Friend that sticks closer than a brother, just as the Scriptures say (see Proverbs 18:24).

I had an encounter with the Holy Spirit personally at En-Gedi, the place where King David hid when Saul was trying to kill him. The Feast of the Tabernacles is an event that the Jewish people celebrate in Israel every year. We had a visitation from the Holy Spirit and it has changed my life completely. I can now say with Job, "I know that my Redeemer lives" (Job 19:25), because of what took place there.

I am totally renewed, so much so that even when I go jogging (which I usually do three times a week), since coming back from Israel, when I get tired the Holy Spirit strengthens me. I try to jog for two hours and when I start tiring, I sing in a beautiful heavenly tongue that the Lord has given me. My whole countenance changes and I physically feel strengthened and relaxed. I don't even feel the pain that comes after running long distances.

Another example is when I leave home – as I do quite frequently to preach the gospel – Jill doesn't come with me because she is an intercessor. She can't keep up with me in the "rat race" of a life that I live. It's anything but glamorous and, as I've said, I do get lonely being away from her.

Since I've had this new encounter with the Holy Spirit, I don't feel as lonely and I don't feel fearful at all when Jill is left on the farm all by herself. I know that my Lord Holy Spirit is with her, just as He is always with me. He is the third person in the Holy Trinity and we really need to cultivate our relationship with Him. The best way to do that is to spend time with Him in His presence. And that is where we come back to our quiet time. When we have an intimate relationship and fellowship with the Holy Spirit, we get to know Him and hear His still voice speaking in our hearts. We learn to know His character – the things He would approve of and the things He doesn't like.

The more time you spend with God, the better you get to know Him, and the stronger your relationship with Him will be. In *Nearing Home*, Billy Graham talks about going home, and he says that we can actually prepare for old age by developing our relationship with God. If our loved ones do go home ahead of us, we will find that we are not as devastated as we might otherwise be.

Some people cannot spend five minutes on their own and they start to panic. I have come to a stage where I just love to spend time with the Holy Spirit. Sometimes Jill has to come and get me out of my quiet time room and tell me to go and do something else, because she is all for a balanced life. I feel this way too, but my relationship becomes so sweet and so intense that it's an absolute pleasure to be on my own with God. Andrew Murray wrote, "Oh the thought of having God all alone to myself and knowing that God has me all alone to Himself!"

Never too busy to talk

It is remarkable to think and to know that the Lord, the Maker of heaven and earth, the busiest Person in creation, is prepared to come and sit for a couple of hours and speak with us. There is no one busier than Him; He is in charge of the entire universe and all the other ones that we don't even know about, and yet He is willing to listen to us and hear about our expectations, our visions, our dreams, and also our fears and shortcomings. It is something truly magnificent.

Can you imagine if your hero – whether a famous athlete, a pop star, or a politician – said they were coming to visit you for a few hours? How would you react? I can assure you, you'd be dressed in your finest clothes; you'd ensure there were no telephones ringing; you'd put up a big sign telling people you were busy; you'd take no interruptions whatsoever because you'd want to give your hero your absolute and undivided attention.

Well, the Creator of heaven and earth *is* wanting to have fellowship with you every single day. And He is such a gracious God, He is even prepared to take your leftovers. Even if you give Him only half an hour, He will gladly take it. The amazing thing is that we are prepared to give time to other people, some of whom we don't even know, but when it comes to the One who died on the cross for us, the One who gave us eternal life, the One who gave us new hope, the One who cancelled all our sins, we are often too busy to speak to Him. We need to rectify this if we want to have a life that is full and abundant.

Loneliness

Loneliness is one of the worst situations to be in while walking the road of life. This book is about facing up to reality; it is not a "froth and bubbles" book, about "pie in the sky". I am trying to be as honest as possible with God and myself, and hopefully it will be of assistance to you.

Super-spiritual people have said to me that a Christian should never be lonely if they know Jesus as Lord and Saviour. I disagree, because even the Master Himself was desperately lonely in the Garden of Gethsemane. He asked His disciples to stay awake and pray with Him, even for an hour, but they couldn't. Thus, it is very possible for a believer to be lonely.

I heard a heart-wrenching story of an elderly widow staying all alone in a little flat in one of those high-rise skyscrapers in one of the major cities of the world. Allegedly, the milkman saw that the woman hadn't collected the milk from her front door for a week. The bottles were piling up, so he called the police. They broke in to find the old soul lying dead in her bed. There was a notebook on her bedside table and every entry each day for the past month read, "No one came today". In the coroner's report, the cause of death was listed as "loneliness".

People who have regular quiet time are never really lonely. One of my biggest inspirations was "Aunty" Peggy O'Neil. She was our intercessor for many years at Shalom Ministries. She was an elderly woman who was physically handicapped: She lost one leg from the knee down because of sugar

> People who have regular quiet time are never really lonely.

diabetes; she had trouble with blood pressure; she had had cancer; and many other illnesses. And yet I never ever saw her as lonely. Eventually she moved to a retirement home in Greytown because she needed specialised care. I would visit her as often as I could.

Whenever I would visit with her in her small room, big enough only for one bed and a chair, she always had her Bible right next to her. I never saw her in her last days ever looking as if she were lonely; she was so at peace. It always felt like if you went into her room, there was more than one person there. She had lots of company, and I'm sure a few angels were there for her too. Most of all, though, the Holy Spirit was her Comforter. Because she had lost her husband many years before (Bob had gone to be with the Lord quite some time previously), she was quite comfortable on her own. The reason was because she was never alone – she had her Friend who sticks closer than a brother, the Holy Spirit.

Developing relationships

As you read this book, you might be a comparatively young person, and I want to encourage you: I want to urge you to develop that relationship with our Lord Holy Spirit. As you do this, you will be investing in your pension for your old age, because, like Billy Graham, whose loved one, Ruth, has gone to be with the Lord, the fact that he has a living relationship with the Lord Holy Spirit is what keeps him comforted.

Just the other day, I spoke to someone who is close to Graham and they said that he is battling with his hearing and even his sight, but that he is still at peace. If you pick up a copy of his book *Nearing Home*, the front cover shows a photograph of Graham. He is sitting and reading his Bible, quite clearly a man who is familiar with being on his own for long stretches of time.

I too am familiar with hotel rooms, motel rooms, the homes of people I do not know well, and aeroplane flights where I spend lots of time on my own. Of course the next extreme is to be in the presence of multitudes of people, so it's a real see-saw, rollercoaster life that I seem to be living at the moment. The only thing that keeps me sane is my quiet time with Jesus. It is definitely not something that is hard for me to do. After preaching for long periods of time I actually hunger for time on my own in the quietness of a room where I can just speak to the Holy Spirit. I talk to Him and, more importantly, allow Him to speak to me and encourage me.

> The only thing that keeps me sane is my quiet time with Jesus.

A living relationship

A man who was very comfortable with being on his own in the presence of the Holy Spirit was a Zulu preacher by the name of William Duma. He was a man who would do nothing without seeking the counsel of God, something he would do before making any decision. He was invited, together with a number of other preachers, to go to Israel as a small gift for his contribution towards the spreading of the gospel. The other preachers accepted the kind invitation and were so excited, literally packing their bags. William Duma, however, asked if he could respond to the organizers the next day, as he first wanted to ask his Lord Holy Spirit about whether he should go or not.

This is the kind of relationship that sustains a person when they get older and their loved ones depart ahead of them for heaven: an intimate friendship with God. As we grow older, we learn to become more patient, to wait upon the Lord. This we find much easier to do than when we were young. It is also because of our physical limitations: we are not as strong as we used to be and carry ailments that tend to slow us down. There is nothing like a little discomfort to slow a person down and keep them humble!

Waiting on the Lord

Many of us struggle in our quiet time to hear from God because we are not prepared to wait for an answer. The Lord sometimes does not even reply to our requests. That is also an answer – it means, "Wait, I am going to come back to you on that one." In this modern world we are continually challenged by time – everything has to be done immediately and it teaches us to be very impatient.

> Many of us struggle in our quiet time to hear from God because we are not prepared to wait for an answer.

When I go into central Africa to preach to our African brethren, I am always amazed at the beautiful way in which Africans wait with such grace. In rural areas, they might wait many hours for a bus or taxi to arrive. In the Western world, people get upset if a train is even five minutes late.

We need to be prepared to wait for the Holy Spirit to speak to us in our quiet times to get the right answer before we go into the battlefield. The Scripture of Isaiah 40:31 is very well known: *"Those who wait on the Lord shall renew their strength."* There are many believers walking around who are totally wounded and ineffective because they are not prepared to wait upon the Lord.

As we get older, we become more adept at waiting to hear from God. As we age, when we do something once, it has to be done correctly, because we don't have the strength to do it ten times over like we used to do when we were young and impulsive.

I don't know about you, but sometimes I would do the same thing a number of times to get it right. I can't do that anymore – I need to wait upon the Lord, get clear instruction from Him, and then to do it once and once only – positively and correctly.

Jesus was never, ever late for an appointment. He was never early either; He was always right on time. I think of the account in the Bible when Jesus raised Lazarus from the dead – the people thought that Jesus arrived four days late, but He was spot on. That miracle transformed the whole of Bethany and the entire district. It is very important in God's service to hear the voice of the Lord. That often takes time and it could take days in order to get a clear directive from the Lord to fulfil His calling on your life.

Remember what we always say at Shalom: "A good idea is not necessarily a God idea and a need does not justify a cause." We must only do what the Holy Spirit tells us to do, nothing more and nothing less.

Chapter 11

Walking by Faith

Walking by faith is impossible without having regular quiet times with the Master. "Why?" you might very well ask. Well, God's Holy Word is very clear on the fact that "*faith comes by hearing, and hearing by the word of God*" (Romans 10:17).

Whenever I am confronted with a major task to carry out for Jesus, I find myself gravitating towards my booth, desperate to hear a clear word of confirmation from Him. At Shalom we have a favourite saying that goes like this: "You must attempt something which is so big that if it's not from God, it is doomed to fail." This is because when it works, people know for sure that something of that magnitude could never have been achieved without divine help. People must conclude that it was God's hand at work. If there is one thing I have found in my journey with Jesus, it is this: don't ever touch God's glory. The only way we can please God is by faith.

It really encourages me when I hear of young men or women going aside and taking time to receive confirmation, before they tackle a project in faith for Jesus.

Faith is very contagious, just like doubt is, and so to receive more faith, and to grow in faith, we must spend more time in the presence of the faithful One, Jesus

Christ, and in His Word. When you start reading faith-building Bible verses like *"I can do all things through Christ who strengthens me"* (Philippians 4:13), *"Is anything too hard for the Lord?"* (Genesis 18:14), *"My God shall supply all your need according to His riches in glory by Christ Jesus"* (Philippians 4:19), and *"If God is for us, who can be against us?"* (Romans 8:31), you will find your faith becoming stronger.

There is a great difference between that kind of encouragement and the kind you receive from people, who would probably say you are stark raving mad to believe promises that were written so long ago. Indeed, that is why Jesus says, *"Do not... cast your pearls before swine"* (Matthew 7:6), simply because these kinds of people don't understand the principles of faith. They don't understand that in Jesus' economy, two times two equals seven. Or that God always honours the

> It's not good works, but raw faith in Jesus Christ that the Lord rewards.

step of faith (not presumption). I often say to people that when I go home to be with the Lord, I would like the words "God always honours faith" to be engraved on my tombstone, because this is something I have personally experienced in my own life. It's not good works, but raw faith in Jesus Christ that the Lord rewards.

When faith steps in, fear steps out! Whatever significant work I have ever done for God always starts off in my booth. When I come with the vision given me by Jesus, I need to be extremely careful with whom I share it. The kinds of comment one receives from non-believers and Christians who choose a "safe" spiritual journey say things like, "Who do you think you are?", "Where is the money coming from?" and so on.

The amazing thing is that not once has the Father failed me when I have truly sought Him with all my heart. Many a time I have stood on a platform, tears streaming down my face as I see with my very own eyes what God promised me in my booth. He assured me that He could do amazing things through me if I would only believe.

Through what God has done, stadiums have been packed to capacity, expenses fully met, the sick healed, blind people have been given their sight, deaf ears have been unstopped, and disabled people have walked. Even weather patterns have changed, with droughts broken in places desperate for rain.

Doors have opened all over the world for me to preach God's Holy Word. To see with my own eyes reconciliation among different racial groups has been very rewarding. I've had preaching appointments that I could only dream of, like preaching at the Western Wall in Jerusalem, the holiest place on earth for Jewish people. I've spoken to people from different religions, classes, and creeds, from kings to presidents, from the wealthy to the poorest of the poor. What an incredible honour it has been.

Do you know the most exciting thing of all? It is that Father God is no respecter of persons; He uses ordinary people (like me) to do His work. We can achieve so much if we would just come aside, step into our booth, and take time waiting on Him. All the glory to Jesus! I could simply go on and on about His greatness!

> God uses ordinary people to do His work.

There is only one thing that Jesus cannot do, and that is to work through a heart that does not believe. He cannot work through a person who refuses to do what He asks of them, because they just will not believe it's possible.

My prayer for every person who reads this book is that they may start spending quality and quantity time each day in their booths waiting to hear God speak to their hearts, building them up in faith so that they can truly tell the mountain to be thrown into the sea!

Dew from heaven

Recently, during my early morning devotions, I read a beautiful story out of the wonderful devotional *Streams in the Desert*. In it, a Dr Pardington writes about the absolute importance of early morning dew on farmlands, flowers, and grasses. I can really vouch for that because, as a farmer, I cannot count the times I have been saved from total crop failure because of that precious, God-sent, early morning dew! I've been growing seed maize for over thirty years (an extremely expensive crop to grow, with huge input costs) on dry land, with no irrigation. We have had to depend entirely on every drop of moisture to be sent from heaven. Maize is designed by God in such a way that its leaves collect moisture and funnel the dew down to the base of the maize stalk for the roots to take it all in – most ingenious.

In order for the dew to settle each night, the conditions must be perfect: no wind or excessive heat. Likewise, he says, the same conditions apply to the Christian who needs

> Heavenly dew is the difference between feeling full of energy, and feeling worn out and bone weary.

life-giving spiritual dew in order to live. Even as physical dew keeps plants alive, so spiritual dew is needed to keep Christians spiritually alive. Many believers do not realize the need for this early morning dew in their lives – that's why they are withered and weary. Yes, it's spiritual renewal we need, and we find it in early morning dew.

Not partaking of this dew, says Pardington, is like a foolish labourer who thinks he can work all day without food. Well, the same thing applies to a servant of God, who thinks he can minister without eating and drinking of that heavenly manna each day. We cannot have spiritual nourishment occasionally – we need renewal from the Holy Spirit *every* day.

Linger longer

Heavenly dew is the difference between feeling full of energy, and feeling worn out and bone weary. It is in quietness and stillness that we receive the spiritual dew from heaven, just like natural dew. We need to wait quietly for our blessed Holy Spirit to send His dew each day.

As plants open their pores each day before the blistering sun arrives, they receive an invigorating "bath". So too do we Christians when we receive that spiritual dew from heaven. By lingering in God's presence, we are totally refreshed. But we must be still before Him, because a heart of haste and disquiet will prevent us from receiving the dew. It is only in stillness and quietness that the moisture from heaven will refresh us. The Father says in Psalm 46:10, *"Be still, and know that I am God."*

It is then that "walking on the water" seems normal, and watching God multiply fish and bread and feeding five thousand becomes another expected miracle. One can literally start living a supernatural life. Unbeknown to us, our faith starts growing. Desperate people bring their sick and tormented loved ones and ask us to pray for them. And yes, God heals them. "Why?" you ask. Because our Father honours prayers of faith – not just prayer, but genuine, heart-rending, faithful prayer.

So as we continue to wait patiently on the Lord Jesus Christ in our booths, He will increase our faith for whatever task is at hand. That is why we see so often, that as God raises up mighty men and women of God for huge tasks, they all gravitate more and more to their booths. Why? It's simple: because that is where they find the faith and strength for the tasks that lie ahead.

My friend Cornelis van Heyningen wrote a beautiful song that became an absolute hit with the Mighty Men™ Conferences we had on the farm. Andy, my oldest son, led the praise and worship each time, and when we sang "In the Stillness of Who You Are" together it felt like the dew from heaven was descending upon us!

I will never forget the oceans of tears I saw from the platform each time we sang it. One man in particular, my best friend, Peter Goosen (who has since been called home to glory after fighting a tough battle with brain cancer), really loved this song. It lifted him every time we sang it together with the multitudes of men. And he would always say to me, "Boet, Jesus says to me, 'My grace is sufficient for you.'" That's how this mighty man of God fought his final battle – by spending time in the stillness and peace of God in his booth, which was a little cottage at the bottom of the garden.

The lyrics of this precious song go like this:

In the stillness of who You are
There I find peace,
In the stillness of who You are
I see Your heart,
In the stillness of who You are
There I find peace,
In the stillness of who You are
I know that You know.

That You know my name
That You know my life
Still You love me, my Lord
Still You care for me
I am the dream in Your heart
And You keep me right there
In the fullness of who You are
I know that You know.

Once we establish this kind of relationship with the living God, then our faith soars to new heights, and those mountains in our lives become mere molehills.

Chapter 12

How to Hear from God

There are a number of things we can do to help us hear more clearly from God. The following could be of help to you.

Firstly, change your Bible to a brand-new one every so often, to give you a new perspective on God's Word.

Secondly, with sermon preparation, get your heart right instead of trying to prepare a masterpiece.

Thirdly, meditate on God and His precious Word. The *Oxford Dictionary* says to meditate is to "focus one's mind for a period of time for spiritual purposes". This can be done in many different ways, such as listening to inspirational gospel music or going for a walk in nature. We are so concerned about our physical health, but how concerned are we about our mental and spiritual well-being? In this busy environment in which we live, we desperately need to give our minds a complete rest, and we need to do it consistently.

> We are so concerned about our physical health, but how concerned are we about our mental and spiritual well-being?

Fourthly, bear in mind that conversational (prayer) time with Jesus is spending time with your best Friend. Never turn your back on God. If you have issues, then you need to voice them to the Father, but always with the greatest respect. People are always saying how they fear the devil, but the truth of the matter is that the person we need to really be sure that we never offend or get on the wrong side of is Jesus Christ! In fact He said Himself: *"Do not fear those who kill the body but cannot kill the soul. But rather fear Him who is able to destroy both soul and body in hell"* (Matthew 10:28).

Lastly, when you are looking for answers, remember this: you will receive them if you are ready and patient enough to wait for them.

This world is desperately looking for role models who will inspire people to great things, but unfortunately they are few and far between. Everyone seems to be so caught up with themselves that they have no time for anybody else. Father God has been my Mentor for a good thirty-three years now, and I can honestly say that He has never once disappointed me. That relationship was birthed in The Secret Place, where He strengthens me, rebukes me, and then encourages me to keep on by faith!

Truthfully, if it wasn't for Jesus being my inspiration, I would never have attempted the exploits God called me to! The fact that they were successful, every one of them, and exceeded my wildest dreams, is because of the inspiration of Jesus, through His Holy Word and His presence through the Holy Spirit during my quiet times.

Inspired by God

Jesus cannot inspire you to great things if you are not present, if you are too busy to listen to His game plan for you. Every time any of the great patriarchs did anything remarkable for God, it was always when they spent time alone, waiting on Him. These include Moses and the burning bush, David and his father's sheep, Elijah and the brook at Cherith, and Jesus at Gethsemane. God inspired them to great feats that are known all over the world – even today, thousands of years later.

After the encounter with God at the burning bush, Moses had enough inspiration to go back to Egypt and tell the pharaoh to let his people go. David spent years looking after his father, Jesse's, sheep. He spent time ministering to God with his harp, and fought off lions and bears. Because he was so inspired, the giant Goliath never intimidated David in the slightest. Elijah was a mighty prophet of the Lord. Why? Because God inspired him at the brook at Cherith to do great things.

> If we really desire to become like Jesus, then we need to spend precious and individual time in His presence.

Then we have our Master Himself, the Lord Jesus Christ, who, after asking His Father to remove the cup from Him, said, *"Not My will, but Yours, be done"* (Luke 22:42). Subsequently, the greatest feat in history took place: Jesus took on the hordes of hell. They were defeated by the man on the Cross of Calvary!

We too, like these spiritual giants of the Bible, need only to look to God to be inspired to do great exploits for Him, and to expect great things from Him. It is the people we spend time with that influence our decision making, and ultimately our very lives. If we really desire to become like Jesus, then we need to spend precious and individual time in His presence.

Begin the day with Jesus

Quiet time should be preferably early in the morning. Why? Well, when you spend time with Jesus first thing in the morning, He sets your pace for the day – He influences your attitude and decision making for the day ahead.

Read the following hymn in a prayerful manner. It is so expressive of what I am saying, written many years ago by Horatius Bonar (1808–1889).

Begin the day with God!
He is thy Sun and Day!
His is the radiance of thy dawn;
To Him address thy day.

Sing a new song at morn!
Join the glad woods and hills;
Join the fresh winds and seas and plains,
Join the bright flowers and rills.

Sing thy first song to God!
Not to thy fellow men;
Not to the creatures of His hand,
But to the glorious One.

Take thy first walk with God!
Let Him go forth with thee;
By stream, or sea, or mountain path,
Seek still His company.

Thy first transaction be
With God Himself above;
So will thy business prosper well,
All the day be love.

Spiritual discipline

Many great men and women of the faith accomplished remarkable things for God, like translating the Bible and writing books, well before the sun came up. For me personally, I find the best time is the early hours of the morning, just before the sun comes up. It is so quiet, so peaceful, and it always feels to me like I can hear the voice of Jesus that much more clearly. It is probably because there is no disturbance! But in order to rise extra early in the morning, we need to be that much more disciplined in our personal lives, such as getting to bed at a decent time!

It is no coincidence that our Father uses some people and not others. People have often come and asked me about it. If you look at such people's lifestyles, you will often see that there is no commitment. They can't get up in the morning for a start, or because they start late, they compromise their quiet time with Jesus. They rush through their Bible reading and prayer time, and can't really hear what the Holy Spirit is trying to tell them, so they go out into the world with no game plan, and no inspiration, and become prime targets for disaster.

> In order to rise extra early in the morning, we need to be that much more disciplined.

You will find that if you rise early in the morning and

give God the first fruits of your day, then you will always be ahead, and you have that extra time to really enjoy God's creation: *"Oh, taste and see that the Lord is good"*, just like the Bible says in Psalm 34:8. This is like savouring a good meal, instead of wolfing it down because you are late for your next appointment. As a result, you never even taste the flavour. But having a leisurely meal means you can take your time and really enjoy the good cooking. Food eaten slowly will do your digestive system a lot of good too! How much more so in our quiet time with Jesus?

So what are we saying, then? Well, if we want God to inspire us, we need to get out of bed in the morning, and we need to seek Him first, before anyone or anything else. Then, when we have heard His gentle voice, we can face the day with confidence and vision, knowing clearly where we are going and what God expects from us.

Chapter 13

Wisdom from God

Something that is becoming harder every day in modern society is to be on one's own, without any interruption. It takes a tremendous amount of self-discipline to come aside each day and spend time with Jesus, and to not allow cell phones or anything else to get between us and our time with God.

This is probably the main reason why it is so important to have a physical place that is private, a "booth" of sorts that is not easily accessible to others. If possible, it should have no outside connections like phones, computers, or two-way radios. The only person who should have access is your spouse or other close family member, who will also understand the value of you being alone with God. All of us need to make critical decisions in life, decisions that could affect our loved ones, and even the society in which we live.

> It takes a tremendous amount of self-discipline to come aside each day and spend time with Jesus.

I heard a wonderful story that illustrates just this. Many years ago, when Jill and I had just become Christians, we were at our first conference in Johannesburg. The speaker was from America, a quietly spoken man. I have never forgotten the story he told. I don't remember the speaker's name, but the story is such a good example of a great man of God who refused to make any major decisions without seeking our heavenly Father's approval.

A lesson from Russia

The person in the story was a man named Aniel. He lived in Russia, in the wide open plains, about three hundred years ago. He was the head of a nomadic tribe, which had herds of cattle, sheep, and horses. They were very happy with their lifestyle, living in tents and moving with their herds and flocks. They were a God-fearing people who paid homage to no one but God. This caused trouble for them because the tsar of Russia accused the little tribe of believers of treason, saying they were rebellious. They refused to bow the knee to anyone but the Lord.

Because of this, Aniel and his people were continually hunted by the tsar's mounted Cossacks, who were ruthless and feared by all. However, Aniel and his little band of followers could never be caught. A sentry would be posted on a hilltop with a trumpet, and as soon as he spotted the enemy he would blow the ram's horn. The tribe would literally pull down the camp and move on within minutes, and the cavalry would never find them. The strength of the little tribe was because of its unity, so it was vital that everyone in the camp pull together. The members of the tribe helped each other, and there was no in-fighting or disagreement. Aniel was a master at keeping law and order. He had an intimate relationship with his Saviour, Jesus, and would never make a decision without first going into his booth and hearing from God.

One day all hell broke loose in the camp, and the leaders came to talk to Aniel. They told him there was a thief in the tribe. The person had brought disunity among the people, because they could no longer trust one another. They were all looking at each other with suspicion, not knowing who the culprit was. Aniel retreated to his booth and remained there for three days in fasting and prayer.

After the three days Aniel came out of his booth, summoned the whole tribe, together with the leaders, and severely rebuked them all. This petty crime could cost them their lives, he said, because if there was no unity, then Father God would not bless them and protect them. Aniel said that if it happened again, the thief, when caught, would be stripped down to the waist, tied to a wagon wheel, and thrashed with a bull whip thirty-nine times. With that, he dismissed the people.

There was no stealing after that, but after a time it started all over again. The leaders came to Aniel, ashamed and hardly knowing what to say. When Aniel heard the news, he became gravely concerned about the possible repercussions. He told the leaders to set a trap for the thief and, when caught, to bring the culprit to him. They would make a public example of him so that it would never happen again.

Eventually the thief was caught and brought before the tribe. What confronted Aniel broke his heart, for there before him stood the thief – his 86-year-old mother. The people were also shattered, and felt very heart sore for their leader. Aniel told his people that he would return to his booth and wait on God, and then tell them what God had said.

After a few days a very forlorn and tired man returned, called the tribe together once more, and said, "The sentence will be carried out." The people could barely believe it, knowing that Aniel's elderly mother could never take such a whipping and still live. And the lashes would be taken on a bare back as well!

Aniel had spent time with God, weighed up the complete picture, and realized the severity of the situation. He could not simply dismiss the charge as it would just encourage more division. He couldn't bear to look on as his mother was whipped, so he decided to take the punishment himself.

The question is, do you think Aniel's mother ever stole again, after having witnessed her innocent son being whipped for something he never did? The answer has to be a very definite no! Of course, when we look at the story, it very clearly reminds us of what the Lord Jesus did for you and me on the Cross of Calvary. Therefore how can we willingly sin again?

What I would really like to stress with this story is that this very wise leader did nothing whatsoever – made no decisions – without first seeking God's counsel in his quiet time. That is why he was so effectively used by our Lord.

Chapter 14

Love Relationship

Song of Songs is about love, but without that love relationship with God, all else is in vain. Remember, the main reason for God creating us was so that we could have fellowship with Him. God does not *need* us, but He does *want* us. He created everything we see around us. The Bible states quite clearly that He loves you and me so much that He offered up His only begotten Son, Jesus, who died on the Cross of Calvary. Jesus paid for our sins, so that *"whoever believes in Him should not perish but have everlasting life"* (John 3:16).

Now that's real love, don't you think? What does He require from you and me in return? Quite simply to love Him and keep His commandments – that is all.

A short while before His death, Jesus said to Peter, *"Do you love Me?... Feed My sheep"* (John 21:17). It is believed that this conversation took place at Peter's Landing on the shores of Lake Galilee. It is my very favourite spot in Israel; I imagine that hardly anything has changed in the landscape there since that eventful day. The Master asked Peter this question no fewer than three times (see John 21:15-17). Why do you think He did this? Maybe because Peter denied Jesus three times. There are all sorts of theories, but the bottom line is that it must have been really important for the Son of God to ask the big fisherman thrice.

Love Is a Verb

I believe that God is saying to us in this late hour, "If you really love Me, then get out there and tell people about Me!" You may say, "Well, I'm not really an evangelist", but you don't have to be! Just keep telling people what Jesus means to you! It's simply a case of one hungry beggar showing another where to find food.

Love is a doing word, so don't keep telling your spouse and others that you love them. *Show* them that you love them, tangibly. How? By loving your children, helping others, doing things for your spouse without them having to ask... the list goes on and on. Theodore Hesburgh wrote, "The most important thing a father can do for his children is to love their mother." How very true indeed. That's the kind of love Jesus expects to see from us. It's our love affair with Jesus that motivates us to love our spouse and children, the widows and orphans, and the homeless person in the street.

> Just keep telling people what Jesus means to you!

But there is also the personal love relationship that every believer has with their Saviour, and that's what we are going to dwell on for a brief moment.

Love God, love people

People have often asked me how I speak to and interact with God. Well, I liken it to the first time I took out my dearest Jill on a date, over forty years ago. First of all, I just couldn't believe that this fine-looking young girl would want to go out with a wild young farmer like me, just recently returned after having been in Australia for a year. I had not a penny to my name. *What interest could she possibly have in me?* I wondered. And yet she did.

When a man or woman meets the Son of God, it is often the same: *What could the Lord Jesus possibly want with a sinner like me?* And yet He does, my dear friend. He desperately wants to talk to us, to love and to help us, to cherish us. It brings to mind the following hymn by Isaac Watts:

> *Were the whole realm of nature mine,*
> *That were a present far too small;*
> *Love so amazing, so divine,*
> *Demands my soul, my life, my all.*
>
> *To Christ, who won for sinners, grace*
> *By bitter grief and anguish sore,*
> *Be praise from all the ransomed race*
> *Forever and forevermore.*

Yes, I was extremely nervous when I met Jill for the first time, which was at a twenty-first birthday party. I asked her if we could go out together for a meal sometime, and she agreed. That was the start of the most wonderful human relationship I have ever known.

A heavenly love affair

The same thing applies when you meet Jesus. Then comes the courting part of the relationship – it's a love affair, no doubt about it. I am more in love with Him, the Creator of heaven and earth, than ever before.

Spending time talking to that special person is a discipline. You need to talk to them with your heart, not your head, while also learning to listen (for me this is extremely hard!). When a person is on their own, they tend to be somewhat self-centred, but once a person has someone else in their life, they need to focus their attention on the other person, not always themselves.

Normally two people come from totally different backgrounds, so it takes great adjustment. It takes time – lots of time! Talking to God, and learning to hear from Him, takes time. A meaningful relationship takes a lot of time to mature and grow, just like marriage.

I feel particularly close to God when I go out and ride my horse, Snowy. I feel the cool breeze on my face, I watch the cloud formations in the distance, I see the wild animals, the birds flying overhead, and of course I'm enjoying being with my horse. This is when I feel totally relaxed. I unwind, and then I start talking with God.

This is similar to how a man would take his girlfriend out on a date. The two of you would sit together and just spend time together, even if you're not saying anything. This is all part of falling in love. You would sit and look at each other, so taken are you by your love's beauty. You are swept off your feet, and a little in awe of being in her presence. That's often how it is when you talk with God – it seems a bit overwhelming, and that, my friend, is the miracle of it all.

I still struggle to come to grips with the fact that the Creator of the universe could take time out of His very busy schedule to speak to me, a sinner saved by grace, who doesn't even know how to address Him correctly.

Aren't we blessed?

Chapter 15

Waiting on God

Waiting on the Lord is probably the most important exercise in all of Christianity, a truth that cannot be stressed strongly enough. St Augustine said, "Patience is the companion of wisdom." Patience comes by waiting on the Lord, which explains why the devil is so determined to keep us as busy as possible. He knows that when we wait on our Father, we become wise men and women.

At the same time, waiting is also one of the most difficult disciplines in the Christian walk. If we go through the Bible, it is evident that the patriarchs – each and every one – had to wait patiently before God used them to carve out His destiny for the world.

If we look at the story of the flood and the ark, Noah built that massive ship by sheer faith, a feat which took decades to do. Abraham waited for about twenty-five years before the Father's promise of a son and an heir became a reality. What about Moses, banished to the wilderness for forty years? It was a long time to wait before God called him to go and deliver the children of God from the pharaoh's clutches. Jesus Himself waited for thirty years before God released Him into ministry. It lasted for only three years, but it changed this world like no man has since, or ever will!

There is a very well-known Scripture in Isaiah in the Old Testament, which so many believers treasure: *"Those who wait on the Lord shall renew their strength; they shall mount up with wings like eagles, they shall run and not be weary, they shall walk and not faint"* (Isaiah 40:31). Wherever I travel these days, I find wounded people; if they are not physically sick, then they are mentally exhausted. There are those who are downcast, bereaved, totally defeated, or without hope; while others feel completely condemned by a sin in their lives. These are the people that Jesus came for, and the remedy is one word: "tabernacle".

Jesus, the tabernacle

Jesus wants to be a tabernacle for you and me. The Word of God says much about the purpose of the tabernacle. For example, Isaiah 4:6 says that *"there will be a tabernacle for shade in the daytime from the heat, for a place of refuge, and for a shelter from storm and rain."*

It's very hard, some might say almost impossible, to renew our strength if we are not familiar with our booth.

> We need to allow the Son to heal us, to deal with those hurts.

When the mighty eagle is sick or wounded, he doesn't go down to the market place, where there is noise and distractions. No, he does the exact opposite – he flies high up into the mountains where the craggy peaks are, and finds a place to rest. There is no one there, only the wind and the rolling clouds passing by. There he spreads his huge imposing wings, and rests in the warm sunshine, allowing his healing to take place.

Dear reader, we so badly need to do the same, just like the mighty eagle. We need to come apart to the "tabernacle". We need to allow the Son to heal us, to deal with those hurts, wounds, misunderstandings, pain, and suffering, whether physical or spiritual.

Nothing will renew our strength like waiting on God. It will give us a new perspective of our situation and we will start to look at it through eyes of faith instead of from a human perspective. In God's economy, our mountains will be reduced to little hills.

I think one of the greatest dangers of serving God is to start taking counsel from other people. Each one, while meaning well, will give you what they think you need to hear, and that can cause utter confusion. Let me clarify what I mean by that statement. We are not talking about godly counsel here; no, we are talking about people's opinion, and when we try to please people, it becomes even more complicated.

Jesus never, ever confuses an issue, He actually simplifies the problem. However, in order to hear that still, quiet voice, we need to come apart, like the eagle, and ensure we hear Him clearly. Then the Son of God will heal us, direct us, and give us freedom from the snares of this life. These things, if we don't take action against them, will drive us over the edge. With weariness comes depression, and a person ends up with no vision, no motivation, and no purpose.

Finishing strong

Hard work, vision, and going for it wholeheartedly does not make a person tired – it is what gives us the strength to not faint but finish strong. It is what gets us up in the morning and motivates us to keep going.

My late dad, now with Jesus, had a heart like a lion. He was without doubt the strongest man I ever knew (a genuine old-fashioned blacksmith). When his best friend in all the world – his beloved wife – was called home to heaven at a comparatively early age, he literally threw the towel in and gave up living. She was simply everything to him. Slowly but surely we saw that wonderful father of ours fade away to nothing, and finally he passed away.

Some people see retirement as an ending of sorts and may even be tempted to give up. Not so for "eagle" Christians. They regroup, recalculate, sharpen their talons. Then, after a season of rest, mourning, and healing, they get back into the race of life, waiting for vision from God.

This is where that beautiful Scripture from Isaiah (*"Those who wait on the Lord..."*) is especially relevant – it emphasizes the importance of having a booth, and how crucial it is to "come ye apart" on a regular basis, just like our Master did when He came to earth. Jesus often went aside and spent time waiting on His Father, for He needed His strength renewed.

In the English Standard Version of the Bible, the commentary says that the meaning of "wait for the Lord" is "savouring God's promise by faith until the time of fulfilment". And again, the meaning of the word "renew" is "to find endless supplies of fresh strength". Human strength, even at its greatest, inevitably fails. Only the promise of God can sustain human perseverance.

Hardship develops patience

In a beautiful book written by Andrew Murray, that amazing man of faith, he talks about patience. He says that the Latin meaning for the word "patience" is suffering. If you think about it, it is only through suffering that we become patient. Paul says in Romans 5:3–4, *"glory in tribulations, knowing that tribulation [suffering] produces perseverance; and perseverance, character; and character, hope."*

A person one might describe as "salt of the earth" is someone who has endured suffering and hardship. So if you ask the Lord to give you patience, He may well bring you suffering. The most impatient people I meet in my life tend to be those who have never suffered. Often they are people who were successful at school, always did well at sport, and were never short of money – things come so easily to them, it seems normal. Accordingly, they get very impatient when things don't go their way.

Let me give you a practical illustration. When you are driving along the highway and your car breaks down, who is the first person to stop? Yes, it's almost always a poor person in an old beaten-up car. Why? Because they know what it's like to suffer, because they have had breakdowns in the past and can sympathize with your predicament. More often than not, the person driving the fancy sports car will just drive straight on. Or he may hoot at you because you've been inconsiderate enough to break down and you're blocking a lane. They would never think that you didn't do it on purpose (and yes, if you had the money, you would buy a new vehicle!).

I have fond memories of when Jill and I started farming. We had literally nothing to begin with, and I remember that for the first three weeks, we lived on potatoes because we had no money to buy any meat! It makes you very patient with others after enduring trying times like these; there is no doubt that hardship develops patience.

Patience is a virtue

If you are going to have proper quiet time with the Lord every morning and you want Him to speak to you, you have to learn to be patient. He will not speak to you in a rush – the Lord is very specific about what He wants to say and how He wants to say it. He doesn't want to share you with anybody else; He doesn't intend playing second fiddle. So if you have other thoughts on your mind, you need to sit quietly, be patient, and focus on the things of God. Then He will start speaking to you through His Spirit, through the Word, through praise and worship, and through prayer. And that takes patience. Sometimes it is hard to settle down, especially for a person like me who is very impulsive by nature. But we do need to be quiet and do nothing and listen for God. This is something that will only come through spending time waiting on Him.

> If you want Him to speak to you, you have to learn to be patient.

Isaiah 40:31 is a Scripture that is so specific, isn't it? *"Those who wait on the Lord..."* This Bible verse is so very true. Have you ever noticed how older people move slower than young people? They are far more specific and careful when they do a task. Why is that? Yes, they don't have the energy that a young person has, but they also tend to do things properly the first time – they don't have the strength to do it twice.

Again Peggy O'Neil, our prayer warrior, comes to mind. As mentioned, she had to have one of her legs amputated because of diabetes. She also suffered from a number of other ailments, yet despite these difficulties, I've never met such a patient lady in all my life. She would spend hours and hours, in fact days on end, praying for the lost, praying for protection over me and my family, praying for the campaigns I was involved in. Sometimes I could almost tangibly feel her pray.

My first duty when I got home from a campaign was to go and to give her an in-depth report. Peggy wanted to know everything in detail, and I remember her patiently writing out everything I told her. "And where are you going next?" she would ask, "How long, and what are you going to be doing, and who's going with you?" She would do her research about that area and find out all about it. Ministry, as we know, is what Jesus Christ Himself was called to in the last few years of His life. He is also an intercessor, and He is interceding on our behalf as I write this book. The power of prayer cannot be underestimated.

> The power of prayer cannot be underestimated.

Patience is indeed a virtue and if we are going to be virtuous men and women who hear from God, we need to give Him time to speak to us – we need to be patient.

Not long ago, my son Fergie asked me to ride with him up to a hill on the farm where we keep some new calves. When we got there, we saw that one of them had an eye infection. Fergie wanted to bring the animal back to the homestead so that he could treat it. He and I were on horseback and one of the boys from the children's home was with us, a young lad about fifteen years of age. It was easy to see how lively he was – so full of energy. He wanted so much to help Fergie and me. But in his enthusiasm and lack of patience, he caused the young animal to become stressed and fearful. The more the animal tried to run away, the faster he would ride after it, until I had to tell him just to stop and leave the animal alone.

After a while, the animal settled right down and we were able to just walk the calf all the way home. He was put in the handling facility and Fergie doctored his eye. Through this I saw how impulsiveness sometimes doesn't help a situation; it makes it worse (especially if you work with animals!). If you are calm and quiet, the animal will usually be the same. It is when we start to rush things that an animal gets uptight and can sense that something is wrong. Then he will want to bolt, and then of course you have a massive problem on your hands. Often this can result in the animal getting injured – by falling or running into a fence. Being patient and then walking slowly behind him and guiding him along always works better. Again, this comes with time and experience. To begin with, I was the worst candidate! I was a very impatient person by nature and would go "like a bull in a china shop" in anything that I did. This often resulted in having to do something three or more times before I got it right. We do need to learn from our mistakes!

One of the biggest tests of my life was when I lost my little nephew, which I describe in an earlier chapter. Having to face his father and mother really took the stuffing out of me. It took away a lot of my confidence and I was reluctant to attempt anything for a long time after that. What it did teach me, though, was to lean on God. It taught me to listen to the voice of the Holy Spirit and it also taught me to say no. They say it takes more faith to say no than to say yes and up until then I had very much been a "people pleaser". I didn't want to offend people and I wanted them to like me. But after that ordeal, I started to realize that whether people liked me or not was unimportant; what was important was being obedient to God.

Be a corner post to the world

I have always said to my children, "People don't have to like you, but they must respect you." And people only respect you if your "yes is yes, and your no is no". A person needs to be steady, reliable, and steadfast, just like a corner post. A corner post is a solid part of a fence – if there is no corner post, the fence will not stand up straight. And how we need corner posts in the kingdom of God today! Men and women who are solid and are like the oak tree that will not be swayed, who are prepared to wait and hear from God be-fore they make an impulsive decision – those are the men and women we need in society today. There is a security about such people, and it all comes back to having a steady quiet time with the Lord.

> How we need corner posts in the kingdom of God today!

If you examine the patriarchs in the Bible, they were individuals who thought before they spoke, who considered things carefully before they took action. They were people whom God could rely on. Moses was one such man. When he was a prince and an heir to the throne of Egypt, he was a self-opinionated, impulsive man, so much so that he killed one of the slave drivers in a rage. As we know, he had to run for his life. But with that time in the wilderness looking after his father-in-law's sheep, he quieted down and became a patient person. When God called him to set His people free, Moses was reluctant to do it. That is what the Lord often does – when we offer our services, He often rejects them, because our motives are impure and we're too erratic. But when we think we're inadequate, that is when He often decides to challenge us and give us a task to do for Him. Quiet times will make you a patient man or woman of God.

Without doubt, it is a discipline to get up in the morning and have your quiet time, sometimes not hearing the voice of God in your heart for days or weeks, but not being concerned about it. Reading the Scriptures, writing them down (in the first person if you so choose), praying, listening to gospel music, and just meditating are wholesome ingredients of a quiet time, and pleasing to the Father. Keeping faithfully to this pattern will make you a patient person, and take all that impulsiveness out of you. Then, and only then, will you be ready for the work that God has called you to.

Also by Angus Buchan

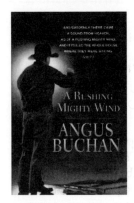

A RUSHING MIGHTY WIND

Angus Buchan's telling of the miraculous events which accompanied his speaking at the Feast of Tabernacles in Israel in September 2012.

ISBN 978 0 85721 555 0 | £7.99 | $14.99

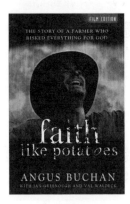

FAITH LIKE POTATOES
THE STORY OF A FARMER WHO RISKED EVERYTHING FOR GOD

Angus Buchan is a straight-talking South African farmer of Scottish extraction. His bold faith has carried him through droughts, family tragedies, and financial crisis. He has seen wonderful miracles of provision and healing.

ISBN 978 1 85424 740 7 | £8.99 | $13.99

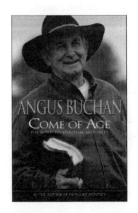

COME OF AGE
THE ROAD TO SPIRITUAL MATURITY

Angus Buchan shot to international attention in the wake of the book and film *Faith like Potatoes*. Now in this new book, he brings his story up to date.

ISBN 978 0 85721 021 0 | £8.99 | $14.99

A Farmer's Year
DAILY TRUTH TO CHANGE YOUR LIFE

A fine companion volume to *Faith Like Potatoes*, offering reflections about the Christian path of discipleship. Simple yet profound daily reflections for people in every walk of life.

ISBN 978 1 85424 850 3
£11.99 | $16.99

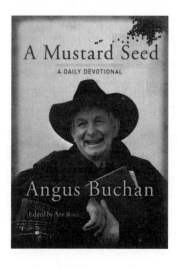

A Mustard Seed
A DAILY DEVOTIONAL

A beautifully-produced 366-day devotional offers daily readings, with a Scripture passage for each day, a meditation (often including an arresting anecdote) and a short prayer.

ISBN 978 0 85721 126 2
£12.99 | $19.99